D0420844

Please return/renew this item by the last date shown on this label, or on your self-service receipt.

To renew this item, visit **www.librarieswest.org.uk** or contact your library

Your borrower number and PIN are required.

Libraries**West**

4 4 0012064 2

33 1/3 Global

33 1/3 Global, a series related to but independent from **33 1/3**, takes the format of the original series of short, music-based books and brings the focus to music throughout the world. With initial volumes focusing on Japanese and Brazilian music, the series will also include volumes on the popular music of Australia/Oceania, Europe, Africa, the Middle East, and more.

33 1/3 Japan

Series Editor: Noriko Manabe

Spanning a range of artists and genres-from the 1960s rock of Happy End to technopop band Yellow Magic Orchestra, the Shibuya-kei of Cornelius, classic anime series *Cowboy Bebop,* J-Pop/EDM hybrid Perfume, and vocaloid star Hatsune Miku—**33 1/3 Japan** is a series devoted to in-depth examination of Japanese albums of the twentieth and twenty-first centuries.

Published titles:

Supercell's *Supercell* featuring Hatsune Miku by Keisuke Yamada;

Yoko Kanno's *Cowboy Bebop Soundtrack* by Rose Bridges

Forthcoming titles:

Cornelius's *Fantasma* by Martin Roberts

33 1/3 Brazil

Series Editor: Jason Stanyek

Covering the genres of samba, tropicália, rock, hip hop, forró, bossa nova, heavy metal and funk, among others, **33 1/3 Brazil** is a series devoted to in-depth examination of the most important Brazilian albums of the twentieth and twenty-first centuries.

Published titles:

Caetano Veloso's *A Foreign Sound* by Barbara Browning

Forthcoming titles:

Tim Maia's *Tim Maia Racional Vols. 1 &2* by Allen Thayer;

João Gilberto and Stan Getz's *Getz/Gilberto* by Brian McCann

Perfume's GAME

Patrick St. Michel

Noriko Manabe, Series Editor

Bloomsbury Academic
An imprint of Bloomsbury Publishing Inc.

B L O O M S B U R Y

NEW YORK · LONDON · OXFORD · NEW DELHI · SYDNEY

Bloomsbury Academic

An imprint of Bloomsbury Publishing Inc

1385 Broadway
New York
NY 10018
USA

50 Bedford Square
London
WC1B 3DP
UK

www.bloomsbury.com

**BLOOMSBURY and the Diana logo are trademarks
of Bloomsbury Publishing Plc**

First published 2018

© Patrick St. Michel, 2018

Library of Congress Cataloging-in-Publication Data
A catalog record for this book is available from the Library of Congress.

ISBN: HB: 978-1-5013-2589-2
       PB: 978-1-5013-2590-8
       ePub: 978-1-5013-2592-2
       ePDF: 978-1-5013-2591-5

Cover image: Photo by Sports Nippon/Getty images

Series: $33\frac{1}{3}$ Japan

Typeset by Deanta Global Publishing Services, Chennai, India
Printed and bound in the United States of America

To find out more about our authors and books
visit www.bloomsbury.com. Here you will find extracts,
author interviews, details of forthcoming events, and
the option to sign up for our newsletters.

Contents

Track Listing

1. "Polyrhythm" (4:09)
2. "Plastic Smile" (4:36)
3. "Game" (5:06)
4. "Baby Cruising Love" (4:41)
5. "Chocolate Disco" (3:46)
6. "Macaroni" (4:39)
7. "Ceramic Girl" (4:34)
8. "Take Me Take Me" (5:28)
9. "Secret Secret" (4:57)
10. "Butterfly" (5:41)
11. "Twinkle Snow Powdery Snow" (3:49)
12. "Puppy Love" (4:32)

Acknowledgments

First, I would like to express my deep gratitude to Bloomsbury Publishing for the opportunity to write this book. Many thanks to Kevin Fellezs, who listened to my early ideas for what this book would look like and was always willing to listen when I needed help, and Noriko Manabe, for heading up this entire project and for all of her guidance (and patience).

There are far too many writers and editors deserving of thanks, for direct help over the last few years or simply serving as an inspiration. In particular, though, I would like to thank Hendrik Jasnoch of the blog *One Week, One Band*, who gave me a chance to write about Perfume for seven days back in 2012 on that site, the first time I went long on the group to a large audience. Thanks to Jayson Greene, who commissioned and helped me immensely in writing a profile of Perfume in 2014 for *Wondering Sound*. Thanks to all writers, past and present, at the *Singles Jukebox*, which still has some of the most passionate and inspiring music writing online around. And thanks to all the other music writers at the *Japan Times* and elsewhere in Japan, especially Ian Martin, James Hadfield, Mark Jarnes, W. David Marx, Aoki Ryōtarō, and Teshima Satoru.

Thanks to Shaun McKenna, for giving me my first chance to be a professional writer and without whom none of this would be possible.

Thanks to all friends who kept me sane over the course of writing this book.

Thanks to my family for their love and support.

And most importantly, thanks to Fujisawa Sena, partially for help translating source materials from Japanese to English, but above all else, for always being there.

Notes on Text

Japanese names are written in Japanese style, with family names before given names (e.g., Nakata Yasutaka).

While many of the stylistic marks used for group names and song titles have been kept, typographic distinctions for artist names and album titles have been removed. Most notably, the album that is the central theme of this book is technically written out in all capital letters, as *GAME*. For the purpose of this book, I have opted to use *Game*. Similarly, the group Capsule originally presented its name as Capsule and today write it as CAPSULE.

The book often refers to the members of Perfume by their nicknames, as they are most commonly known in Japan.

Unless specified, translations from the Japanese original are by the author.

Introduction

Japanese pop music leans toward the familiar—a characteristic that has become particularly noticeable since 2000. At the end of every year, the country's top-selling album list always features a handful of best-of compilations, consisting of fancy repackagings of songs that have already been around for a long time. This marketing pattern appeals to older Japanese fans who still purchase CDs, making compilations a safe bet for record labels. Yet familiarity is also a factor. Safely revisiting the past often trumps trying something new; even when major-label artists venture into new sonic territory for J-pop, or update yesterday's sounds to match today's, the sales rarely seem to impress. J-pop leans toward conservative tastes.

But every once in a while an artist captures the attention of fans and critics with a style that does not pander to the existing mainstream. Such styles rarely appear *just* because the music itself is worthy of attention; timing can be just as vital. New music can capture the essence of major shifts in Japanese society, helping it to gain a wider audience. Musical trends are borne of such situations, when something new arises in spite of industry practices that often tend to favor the tried and true.

The year 2008 was a major moment when a new sound lit up the J-pop soundscape. To those not in the know, Perfume looked exactly like the other female performers who had been occupying the J-pop charts for decades. The trio comprises Kashino Yuka, Nishiwaki Ayaka, and Ōmoto Ayano, all better known by their respective nicknames: Kashiyuka, A-chan (pronounced "Aa-chan"), and Nocchi. They formed the group when they were tweens at an acting school in their hometown of Hiroshima. They advertised their group by handing out flyers to pedestrians on the street. At this early stage of their career, Perfume reflected the typical styles of a J-pop girl group: they sang upbeat, chirpy numbers that showed off the full range of their voices (even if they did not hit every note perfectly), and they performed synchronized dance moves in matching outfits.

That was most certainly not the sound found on *Game*, Perfume's first official full-length album of previously unreleased material. Every song was saturated in synthesizers and drum machine beats. The heaviness of the bass had more in common with French house music than Perfume's pop contemporaries of the aughts (2000–09), more apt for a darkened Parisian club headlined by the Ed Banger All-Stars than the streets and shops of Shibuya. The women's singing was also different. Whereas most J-pop mixes at this time emphasized the vocals, the trio's voices were mixed slightly lower. While other Japanese superstars such as Utada Hikaru and Hamasaki Ayumi sometimes sounded dramatic with their imitated cries, Perfume sounded almost monotone in their delivery, the words melding into the thumping, club-inspired music rather than towering above it. Most strikingly, Kashiyuka, A-chan, and Nocchi's voices were digitally manipulated: they were heavily compressed and run through autotune. The electro-soaked voices did not sound like human voices. They sounded like another instrument in the mix instead of the focus of attention, as with most J-pop stars. *Game* sounded like the future—or, at least, someone's idea of a future, where computers played a central role and everything is extremely sleek.

The album is a front-to-back pop behemoth, full of bouncy verses leading to memorable choruses. Despite the robotic sound, emotion still oozes out of this machine. These songs fixate on classic pop topics, especially love. They comfort high schoolers feeling alone during the winter through the celebration of chocolate. These lyrics hit directly at one's heart. *Game* might be constructed like an aural shot of dopamine, but it also conceals a bittersweet edge, where the uncertainty that follows the thrill of new attraction always lurks in the background. *Game* sounds achingly human, set against this digital backdrop.

Most of the credit for the sound goes to Nakata Yasutaka, the producer behind *Game* and Perfume's music.[1] Influenced by 1980s synth-pop and the radio-ready J-pop of the 1990s, Nakata had captured attention in the early 2000s with the duo Capsule, noted for its cheery pop, influenced by Parisian styles and bossa nova. He soon changed his approach to music, embracing blown-out electropop sounds fit for packing dancefloors. Yet unlike the hedonistic maximalism of Justice or Digitalism, Nakata brought out the human emotions from the digital morass. He created numbers that had a fresh sound but still hit on all the pleasure points of pop, the sort of songs that could grab your attention when you heard it in a store or from a street truck.

Until *Game*, Perfume had struggled to sell many singles or compilation albums, which were always on the outer edges of Japan's various music charts. They performed shows at less-than-noteworthy venues, ranging from the parking lot of a bowling alley to a corner inside an Apple Store. When the group signed to a major label in the mid-aughts, the head of the record company so lacked confidence in them that he recommended that they attend college, just in case.[2]

As their unique style caught the attention of tastemakers and commercial directors, Perfume slowly but surely started gaining the attention of mainstream listeners.

When *Game* was released on April 16, 2008, it debuted at the top of the Oricon weekly album charts, having moved 154,000 copies in its first seven days.[3] It was quite the comeback for a trio that had almost called it quits a year earlier. Perfume also broke some long-standing records with their debut album. By taking the top spot on the charts, Perfume became the first technopop artist to achieve that since the celebrated trio Yellow Magic Orchestra (YMO) did the same in 1983.[4] Plenty of computer-generated music had achieved success in the time before *Game*, but this collection seemed more direct about its digital heritage. Perfume remains J-pop stars today, selling out stadiums in Japan and touring internationally. And they did so by breaking away from conventional sounds.

"I don't think J-pop should be made into a particular genre with its own rules," Nakata told the *Japan Times* in 2011.[5]

A Welcoming Fragrance

Sales figures and chart milestones are only partial indicators of the degree of Perfume's success in the Japanese pop mainstream after the release of *Game*. I came to Japan in the summer of 2009 as part of a program for teaching English. Nabari, my new home on the western edge of Mie Prefecture, felt small enough that I would meet somebody I knew nearly every time I went out. Yet it was also spread out, making trips anywhere beyond the nearby convenience store a serious undertaking.

My chief concern early on was what I would say to people living in Nabari. The novelty of discussing where I was from and what foods I liked wore off quickly, and conversations would then enter an awkward repeating loop of, "Well, great weather today, huh?" In my workplace, I had no idea how to connect with the teens in my classroom, especially when it came to music. Sure, every student could recognize the Beatles's songs; even textbooks included "Yesterday." But what music did they actually enjoy?

A couple of weeks after arriving, I went to a big-box electronics store near my apartment. While browsing aimlessly through the shop, a song came on the in-store sound system that sounded like nothing I had ever heard before. The music was electronic and loud, like the bloghouse songs I had downloaded without hesitation while in college, but instead of a hedonistic ethos, it had a sweet pop core that created a lovely tension alongside the pounding bass lines. I could hear voices within its pulsating frame, but they sounded more android than human. Yet the more I listened—and by this point, I was just standing still in the computer aisle, to the bewilderment of store staff—the more I was overcome by the sheer joy in this song. It sounded computerized, but it was surely powered by the most upbeat operating system ever imagined.

Scouring message boards and YouTube for information and music videos of the group, I found out that people, not some deeply empathetic software, made this music. When my first paycheck hit my bank account about a month later, I went to nearby Osaka and bought all three of Perfume's then-released albums, including *Game*. For a while, it was all I listened to, and those CDs never ended up far away from my computer, even after the initial rush of discovery wore off and I simply became more familiar with them.

Through Perfume, I suddenly had a way to connect with the people around me. *Everybody* knew Perfume, as they had become one of the nation's biggest pop acts. For my teenage students, Perfume was cool, and for the girls, they were even inspiring; they demanded to know which member was my favorite. Once an awkward post-work karaoke session with coworkers actually became fun when one of them selected "Chocolate Disco"; come the hook, all of us had something to shout along in simple English. Even in a relatively small city away from a major metropolis, everyone knew about Perfume. And most people liked at least one of their songs. Whether it was because they sounded different from other artists or their songs were especially catchy, people loved to talk about their music. Perfume not only opened the doors for me to my community but also to learn more about J-pop. Perfume—and the songs on *Game*, their biggest moment in the greater field of Japanese pop culture—connected me to the country I now called home.

It caught me off guard to realize that Perfume was not an obscure find. It was mainstream J-pop. The three members of the group popped up on my TV screen constantly. Ads featuring them were all over my sleepy town. A song of Perfume was the soundtrack to commercials for fizzy alcohol pop drinks. Many Japanese artists, including Perfume's producer Nakata, made electropop and did it well. But Perfume was the one that everybody knew. And to me, Perfume sounded better than any pop coming from anywhere that year.

Is It Technopop?

After *Game* debuted on the top of the domestic album charts, Japanese media dubbed it the first number-one technopop album in over two decades. Technopop refers to a genre that was popular in the late 1970s and early 1980s; in the West, it would be akin to synth-pop or new wave. The key part of that word is "techno," not as in the soon-to-be-developed dance genre, but as short for "technology." Japanese albums by Isao Tomita among others had previously been made with synthesizers and other electronic instruments, but it was the YMO that first received mainstream attention with songs constructed entirely out of hulking synthesizers, vocoder, and drum machines. Tagged as technopop, synth-centric music became trendy for a few years—computer music for the computer age.

Some fans of technopop bristled at Perfume being labeled as such. Blogs complained that the media had wrongly categorized the group and that the J-pop trio sounded nothing like YMO or any of the other technopop groups of that time. They said it sounded more like Daft Punk than anything else.[6] The skeptical included Sakamoto Ryūichi, one of the members of YMO, who said, "I don't really understand it. It's just the latest fad."[7]

They were right: Perfume was not really technopop. That moniker was tied to a very specific period in Japanese history. As computers and digital music were becoming more common in the late 1970s, the musical style they enabled combined with explorations of the image of Japan (and Asia as a whole) in the West, as exemplified by Hosono Harumi's "Soy Sauce Music" trilogy.[8] In Hosono's next project, the Yellow Magic Orchestra, the parodying of the West's exoticism of Japan transformed into techno-orientalism, described as "the phenomenon of imagining Asia and Asians in hypo- or hypertechnological terms in cultural productions and political discourse."[9]

The music itself was spurred by the relative ease a musician had at this point to buy digital instruments—synthesizers were as big as kitchen cabinets five years earlier, but by 1980, one could buy a miniature synth easily. By the 1990s, this would all seem quaint. Consumer electronics were commonplace, and it would be hard to find a pop song *not* utilizing a computer at some point in its creation. The world where technopop could flourish had moved on.

Perfume and *Game* could never truly be technopop; their appearance as three young female singers would still tie them to J-pop girl groups. But they were the first Japanese group in decades to take the spirit guiding technopop and update it to the technological possibilities and cultural references that had come into being since the 1980s. Like the technopop artists before him, Nakata created *Game* in a way utilizing the latest technology, which in 2008 meant doing everything on his computer; all of *Game* was recorded in a tiny studio that resembled a living room (in fact, the trio's vocals were recorded in a closet), and the latest software allowed him to fine-tune every detail of these songs. These technical affordances were coupled with his songwriting skills and desire to bring something new into mainstream J-pop—a desire that pushed the usually stoic Nakata to fight passionately for the original recordings to be used on the album when the label pressured him for more pop-friendly mixes.

Game also reflected the times, when personalized technology, always big in Japan, had become increasingly multimedia-capable. It is not a coincidence that Perfume's first real success came on Nico Nico Dōga, a popular Japanese video-sharing site that overlaid user comments synchronized to particular spots on the video. This digital pop seemed appropriate for people whose lives were increasingly spent online, looking at their high-tech phones or listening to MP3s on an iPod. Every square inch of Perfume's music sounded electronic and reflective of the near future, down to the three women's voices sounding robotic. Nakata maximized the sounds of these songs, crowding them with different noises and making them loud, and they fit with the emerging age. Listening a decade on, *Game*'s buzziness and at times overwhelming mix seems an apt reflection of an internet-driven world, where content, news, and voices are relentlessly coming in, and silence is a rarity. Perfume did not pioneer this heavy electropop style—as mentioned, Justice and Digitalism had already been pushing dance music into this direction, and the influence of Daft Punk's *Human After All* (2005) can be heard in Nakata's style. Sakamoto was not wrong when he brought them up as a comparison.

While Daft Punk framed technology in a paranoid light, dehumanizing at best and a tool of outright fascism at worst, Perfume sang about technology with a shrug, accepting this new world and ultimately embracing it. Nakata and the three members touched on familiar subjects while drowning them in modern sounds. They were ahead of the curve with *Game*, as a few years later, the overwhelming, emotional branches of electronic dance music (EDM) would be among the most popular styles in the world.

Game is a great pop album that encapsulated the age of highly personalized information and brought a radically new sound to the mainstream charts. But it did not simply emerge from Nakata's cramped home studio. Rather, it was shaped by decades of music, from technopop of the late 1970s, to J-pop of the 1990s, to dance music of the 2000s. It represents the culmination of Japan's long-running intersection of pop music and technology.

1 The Age of Technopop

Isao Tomita went to extreme lengths to bring a Moog synthesizer into Japan. A classical composer writing music for Japanese television shows and movies since the mid-1950s, he had come to the conclusion that every sound possible via orchestration had already been done well before he came of age. Dozens upon dozens of people before him had already exhausted the potential of a classical orchestra, and Tomita had long sought a new instrument, something that could be uniquely his and fulfill his desire not to be simply redoing the past.

He found a lead when he came across Wendy Carlos's *Switched-On Bach* (1968), a collection of the German composer's creations replicated by an American using a Moog electronic synthesizer the size of a living room table. The record had been a commercial hit and was even played at the US Pavilion at the 1970 World Expo held in Osaka (though Tomita had already encountered it by then).[1] The album showed that the synthesizer was more than a novelty but could tackle one of the West's most celebrated artists' music. In its interpretations of Bach, Tomita heard a tool capable of new sonic horizons.

Tracking one down, though, turned out to be a daunting challenge. Tomita could not locate a synthesizer in Japan like the one featured on the cover of *Switched-On Bach*, but he was directed to a distant and frozen corner of the world—Buffalo. Tomita flew out to upstate New York and found the rural town where Robert Moog was building his hulking electronic synthesizers, in a space that struck Tomita more as a shed than a factory. He would come this far, and he was ready to buy a Moog III on the spot, for a total cost that would equal many people's annual income—around ¥10 million (roughly $125,000) in 2012 terms.[2]

The daunting price tag was not the end of Tomita's tribulations, though. Owing to a near lack of electronic synthesizers in the country, Japanese custom officials were left baffled by the gigantic crate that showed up at their offices. Tomita told them it was a musical instrument. Skeptical, they told him to play it in front of them. An acoustic guitar it was not, and the Moog lacked instructions teaching anyone how to operate it. Tomita tried showing them the artwork of *Switched-On Bach*, but to no avail. The instrument sat around in limbo for months before Tomita received a photo from Moog itself of Keith Emerson (of the progressive rock band Emerson, Lake and Palmer) manning the same synthesizer at a live show. That was the proof he needed to take his huge piece of equipment home and set the stage for the arrival of technopop in Japan.[3]

For decades before, Japanese people had been experimenting with machine-made music. National broadcaster Japan Broadcasting Corporation (NHK) established the NHK Studio in 1955, and its artists, such as prolific film soundtrack maker Mayuzumi Toshirō, created some of the earliest electronic music in the nation. Many of these early recordings were more like laboratory experiments, with names such as *Music for Sine-Waves by Proportion of Prime Numbers*.[4] These important developments, however, were hardly the type of music that would capture the attention of thousands upon thousands of people.

Tomita set the stage for the digital dominoes to fall. Once he assembled the intimidating Moog III and figured out how to generate sounds from it, he went to work creating his own style, initially applying the *Switched-On Bach* formula of recreating well-known pieces, but tackling modern pop and rock songs (the Beatles's "Yesterday," Simon and Garfunkel's "Mrs. Robinson") and transforming them into synthesizer-only tunes, complete with computer-generated vocals. It sounded like a novelty—all your favorite songs, gone Moog!—but it was a big step forward for the composer. It set the stage for his pivotal second album, *Snowflakes Are Dancing* (1974), wherein he took his electronic touch to Claude Debussy's tone paintings. The synthesized notes revealed a new dimension to Debussy's work, with Tomita's versions sounding lush and alive. A smash hit, it went on to be nominated for four Grammy awards in 1975.

Matsutake Hideki picked up on the potential of what Tomita was doing. The Yokohama-born Matsutake had long been intrigued by electronic sounds—he, too, had heard new possibilities in *Switched-On Bach* at Expo '70. He served as an apprentice—via a job with a management company—to Tomita starting in 1971, allowing him to observe the composer wrangle with the Moog synthesizer and even play around with it himself when Tomita was not using it.

By the mid-1970s, Matsutake, who had branched out on his own, found himself in the company of Hosono Haruomi—a musician who had played in the influential rock band Happy End. After that band had broken up, Hosono had released several solo albums flirting with exotica, particularly as played by American composer Martin Denny, which offered a fantasy image of Asia and the South Pacific in the stereotypical sounds of pentatonic scales, parallel fourths, and wood percussion. He found himself associating with a budding musician named Sakamoto Ryūichi. Matsutake worked on both of their solo recordings. When Hosono, Sakamoto, and former Sadistic Mika Band drummer Takahashi Yukihiro decided to form YMO, originally conceived as a disco-influenced, one-off project poking fun at the Western world's orientalist view of Asia as exemplified by Denny's creations, Matsutake was pulled into their orbit. To many in the media, he became the "fourth member" of the unit, bringing the knowledge he acquired from working with Tomita to this new project. According to Matsutake, YMO spent much time analyzing Tomita's work; Sakamoto, who owned all of Tomita's records, brought them into the studio and said, "Today, let's listen to this and study [it.]." As Matsutake told *Resident Advisor*, "YMO's sound is definitely rooted in Tomita's music."[5]

YMO made pop music ready for the dance floor, constructed primarily from electronic sounds of the day—synthesizers, video game bleeps, drum machines, and vocoders. Coupled with science-fiction themes and futuristic visuals, YMO caught attention not only in its home country but also abroad. Its single "Firecracker"—a computer-age reimagining of Denny's exotica piece of the same name, the Tiki-Bar atmosphere of the original transformed into a plugged-in disco shuffler—became a hit in the United States. This success overseas helped the group to land advertising tie-ups with Fuji Cassette and Seiko watches, transforming its members into megastars at home.[6]

What started off as a one-album project turned into the most popular musical outfit in Japan for several years, launching a YMO boom. The group's synthesizer-powered sound not only influenced Japanese artists, but reached Afrika Bambaataa in the Bronx and the Belleville Three in Detroit, influencing these pioneers of hip-hop and techno respectively. The band also performed on the American TV show *Soul Train* in 1980, with a playful interview with Don Cornelius. Most importantly, YMO launched a full-blown craze for technopop in Japan, turning the first half of the 1980s into a time when electronic sounds dominated both the mainstream and underground scenes. In just under a decade, electronic music went from something confounding customs workers to a nationwide phenomenon.

Defining Technopop

What exactly is technopop? The term was coined by Japanese music critic Agi Yuzuru in a 1978 review in *Rock Magazine* of the German group Kraftwerk's *The Man Machine*. The descriptor was fitting for this album, which was built entirely out of electronic sounds; it opened with the group repeating, "We are the robots," through vocoder.

"Isn't the pioneer Kraftwerk?" Hosono asked in an interview from 2008, recorded backstage at a special YMO reunion show in London. "Giorgio Moroder," Sakamoto added, "the pioneers are obviously Kraftwerk and Giorgio Moroder." Takahashi closed the interview by saying with a laugh, "The two Germans, Giorgio, and we're third."[7] In an interview with *San Francisco Weekly* in 2011, Sakamoto said, "I introduced Kraftwerk to the other members of YMO and they immediately became huge fans. But instead of imitating Kraftwerk, obviously, we wanted to invent something original—technopop from Japan. Kraftwerk was very German. We wanted to create something very Japanese."[8]

Agi's idea of technopop was not necessarily tied to a specific sound; Kraftwerk's ruminations of mundane aspects of daily life over repetitive, sparse, and hypnotic music may have had little in common with Moroder's dance-floor creations. But both artists embraced the new sounds of electronic synthesizers, along with vocoder and drum machines. The concept of the future seemed embedded in their sounds, with Moroder's synthesized disco cut "I Feel Love" evoking a feeling of the world beyond today, or Kraftwerk's *The Man Machine*, with its references to Fritz Lang's film *Metropolis* (1927), evoking a 1930s imagining of what tomorrow might look like.[9] "Techno" simply stood for "technology."

The emphasis on technology reflected the times. The post–Second World War boom had raised the majority of Japan's citizens comfortably into the middle class. This wealth enabled widespread diffusion of consumer electronic products made by Japanese companies: television sets in the 1960s, JVC's VHS and Sony's Betamax in the 1970s, Sony's Walkman from 1979, and successive generations of video games. As creators of consumer electronics products that were exported worldwide, Japan developed an image internationally as perpetuators of a modern, electronically driven lifestyle. Meanwhile, from the late 1970s onward, Japanese makers like Yamaha, Roland, and Casio began issuing digital synthesizers, drum machines, and other digital instruments, resulting in an increase in synthesized sounds. The Plastics, P-Model, and Hikashū all acquired and featured Roland CR-78 Rhythm Machines in their releases of the late 1970s to early 1980s.[10] Technopop reflected this shift; the ever-present hum of electronic instruments mirrored the way in which electronic devices were becoming more ingrained in daily life.

YMO itself is dubbed a reimport because the attention it received overseas helped it to gain recognition in Japan, pushing technopop into the mainstream. Their second album, *Solid State Survivor,* was the best-selling album of 1980 and produced several Japanese classics, including "Behind the Mask," a vocoder-drenched song about an unemotional future that was covered by Michael Jackson (1982, posthumously released). The band appeared in advertisements for Seiko Watch and FujiFilm, and Japanese electronics retailers played YMO's music in the stores, further associating them with technology. Technopop entered the larger cultural imaginary as the monochrome costumes and stark haircuts of YMO gave way to fashion trends and techno haircuts.[11]

Several bands of the late 1970s who also featured synthesizers were also put under the technopop category, although their philosophies were different. In contrast to the studiousness with which YMO created music with electronics, the Plastics embraced a punk-influenced DIY ethos while their bassist Sakuma Masahide, a former member of progressive rock band Yoninbayashi, introduced them to Kraftwerk. The group toured the United States, performing with the B-52s and Talking Heads. Songs like "Copy" show the group's Devo-like balance of punk energy, electronics, and ironic lyrics, delivered by Nakanishi Toshio and Satō Chika in a clipped vocal style that could sound like malfunctioning droids. Across their celebrated 1979 album, *Welcome Plastics*, they sang about technologic signifiers—TVs, robots, IBM.[12]

P-Model and Hikashū, two other bands that played with synthesizers and a sense of irony, were called technopop by virtue of timing. As singer-songwriter Komuro Hitoshi said on his radio program *Ongaku Yawa* (Music Night Talk), "You use synthesizers and other instruments to create a cutting-edge sound. That's totally a new style of music in vogue, the sound of this age. What you wear, the words you speak, and everything, as well as your music, all of them are created reflecting this age and the present environment." The remarks of Makigami Kōichi, the theremin-playing leader of Hikashū, betrayed his ambivalence to the label: "I think we are just playing the music we want to play. We're like that. But, well, 'Technopop' is probably the easiest thing for people to call our kind of music."[13]

Technopop spurred new artists and existing artists to play with synthesized sounds. It ranged from the intricate synthesized explorations of Matsutake Hideki's Logic System, to the electro-stomp of BGM, a project started by Agi Yuzuru, the writer who coined the term technopop. Takahashi and Hosono established their own sub-label, ¥en Label, under their record label Alfa Records, and Hosono personally produced the eclectic Koshi Miharu and Sandii & the Sunsetz. Technopop was also integrated into mainstream postwar popular song style (kayōkyoku) as techno-kayō, where the voice-centric style was backed by electronic sounds.

One noteworthy entry was Juicy Fruits, a quartet that began as Beef, the backing band for Chikada Haruo. The band's sound was distinguished by Okuno Atsuko's singing, which writers described as "fluffy but monotone."[14] In the group's first and best-selling single "Jenny wa gokigen naname" (Jenny in a Bad Mood, composed by Chikada), Okuno chides her inattentive lover in a high-pitched, cute, but expressionless manner; her robot-like voice matches the twinkling keyboard notes, blending with the instrument. Juicy Fruits's approach proved to be one of the most commercially viable takes on technopop in the early 1980s, with Okuno's cute-but-cold persona matching images of fashionable women at the time.

The song has remained in the cultural imagination and has been covered many times over the decades.

The vogue of technopop peaked in 1983, with the release of YMO's sixth album, *Uwaki na bokura* (Naughty Boys). This collection still featured the electronic-age buzz of their previous work, but was unabashedly radio-friendly, with themes of love and music itself. Its lead single was "Kimi ni mune kyun" (My Heart Skips a Beat for You), a catchy, vocally focused techno-kayō that was used in a Kanebō cosmetics commercial. It was the group's best-selling single. The promotional video also reflected this pop orientation, simply showing the three members dancing—a far cry from the techno-centric imagery of the group's early days. Perhaps this unapologetic pop was a logical endpoint for a group that had achieved a success that they had not anticipated. The members were no longer imagining the near future, but capturing the now. *Naughty Boys* topped the Oricon album charts upon its release—the last technopop album to achieve such a feat for twenty-five years.

Thereafter, technopop lost its luster: as digital technologies in music production became pervasive, the term technopop lost its sense of meaning. Musical trends shifted back to guitar-centric bands in the late 1980s. YMO took some time away, too. After *Naughty Boys*, the group "spread out"; each member pursued solo careers while still collaborating with one another. The group reunited in 1993 to produce the original album *Technodon*. This album made a large impression on a junior high school student with a budding interest in songwriting.

2 Music Controller

Nakata Yasutaka (b. 1980) hails from Kanazawa, a historic city on the Sea of Japan, renowned for seafood and ancient castles. Starting piano lessons at an early age, he was composing his own songs by the age of ten, recording them on cassettes. Like many young Japanese, he played video games and watched TV, which left a deep musical impression on him. The 8-bit beeps and 16-bit sounds fascinated him, as did commercial jingles in the 1980s, some of which featured synthesizers. Nakata's father had an interest in film soundtracks, an influence that may have contributed to the son's preference for instrumental music.[1] As a child, Nakata primarily listened to instrumental numbers, well-known Western acts, and cartoon theme songs.

One such song was "Odoru pompokorin" (Pompokorin Dancing, 1990), the ending theme to the popular animated cartoon *Chibi Maruko-chan* (Little Maruko), with lyrics by the show's creator, Sakura Momoku, and music by Oda Tetsurō. Performed by the group B. B. Queens, it was the best-selling single of 1990. Part of its whirlwind charm lies in the backing vocals at the chorus, which have been run through a vocoder. Nakata admitted that the electronically manipulated singing made a lasting impression on him.[2]

Another awakening for Nakata was *Technodon* (1993), which YMO made after a decade's hiatus. While relying less on sampling than on earlier recordings (due to the greater likelihood of copyright-related lawsuits by the 1990s), the album continued with the techno-orientalist theme, featuring on "Floating Away," a voiceover by cyberpunk author William Gibson, described by David Roh et al. as "the most renowned exemplar of the West's fascination with the technologized Asian subject."[3] The album prompted a revival of interest in YMO, which was featured in magazines like *Sound & Recording*.

By this time, Nakata was a junior high school student who was starting to compose, and he began turning for guidance to technically focused magazines such as *Sound & Recording*. As he said in a 2012 joint interview with Sakamoto Ryūichi,

> I read the issue devoted to YMO and learned about *Technodon*, and I listened to it. I was shocked. . . . I didn't know much about music, but I thought *Technodon* is something I should listen to a lot to understand. It was what I listened to the most while I was in junior high school. I really like the sound of it. I sometimes listen to it to go to bed.[4]

Technodon introduced new listeners to YMO and reminded the music world of the technopop of the late 1970s. It came about a time when Japanese music was changing drastically.

Departures

Sometime in the switchover between the Shōwa Era (1925–89) and the Heisei Era (1989–), Japanese popular music was rebranded from *kayōkyoku*, a vocally focused pop style, to J-pop. The new term implied a high-energy, happy-sounding, sleeker, more globally appealing kind of pop, and the rise of new artists gave the impression of difference from older styles.

One of the most influential figures of 1990s J-pop was Komuro Tetsuya, a producer who first gained attention in the band TM Network in the mid-1980s. Coming at the tail end of the technopop boom, the trio's blend of traditional rock guitar with synthesizer positioned it well when rock bands came back into vogue. As a producer in the 1990s, Komuro blended trendy European dance sounds with pop, introducing dance music into the mainstream and creating the pop-hit formula for the decade. One of his first major commercial triumphs was TRF—the name standing for Tetsuya Rave Factory, with rave referring to European rave, a popular dance club style. His trio Globe matched Euro-pop with dramatic ballads and rapping. Perhaps most famously, he produced the breakout albums for J-pop queen Amuro Namie. Whereas YMO questioned and at times subverted the idea of pop in the late 1970s, Komuro was an unabashed populist, creating songs that the *Los Angeles Times* described in 1997 as "suitable for disco as for karaoke." By 1996, Komuro had record sales of 100 million to his name.[5]

Moving On

When Nakata bought a Yamaha EOS B700 synthesizer, a model released in 1993, he did not know that Komuro himself had designed this instrument for use in producing dance hits.[6] In 1996, Nakata entered XG Sound World, a contest held by Yamaha. He submitted two contrasting original compositions: "Kaiseki ryōri" (Japanese smorgasbord), which simulated the sounds of Japanese instruments such as koto (zither), shakuhachi (bamboo flute), and shamisen (three-stringed lute); and "XGroove," a danceable track with synthesizer melodies, tinny percussion beats, and a jazz-inflected piano line that would have fit in at a dance club blasting Komuro-produced songs.

Nakata won a prize for technique, and he used the prize money to buy a sampler. A year later, while attending a youth-oriented party in Kanazawa, he met Koshijima Toshiko, another Kanazawa native of the same age. They soon started working together on a project called Capsule, where he produced the music and she sang.[7] "She's very flexible," Nakata told the *Japan Times* in the late 2000s, "so whatever I want to do at a particular moment, she'll say, 'Yeah, let's do it.'"[8]

Nakata moved to Tokyo to attend the Tokyo School of Music, a specialized training college catering to the entertainment industry. In 1999, he landed his first professional job, producing music for a J-pop idol group called Tennen Shōjo EX. His two songs had some Komuro-like elements, namely melodic dance music featuring piano and synthesizer, but they also had a softer feel to match the idol-oriented project. Rather than pursue this style, he formed Sync⇔Sync with fellow student Kinoko Emi. Capsule released its first album, *High Collar Girl*, a pop album incorporating elements of traditional Japanese music alongside electronic beats. Rather than the more mainstream pop exemplified by Komuro, *High Collar Girl* and early Capsule were more reflective of Shibuya-kei, another popular style of the 1990s.

While technopop of the 1980s had looked to the future, the sounds of the 1990s tended either to embrace an in-the-moment, lose-yourself attitude exemplified by Komuro's Eurodance-pop, or look to the past. The nostalgic genre was Shibuya-kei (Shibuya style), in reference to the record-store-filled Tokyo neighborhood; its artists, including Flipper's Guitar, Cornelius, Kahimi Karie, and Pizzicato Five, thus consciously separated themselves from the mainstream.[9] Shibuya-kei artists embraced a diversity of old and often obscure styles, with Cornelius paying homage to the Beach Boys, while

Pizzicato Five referenced 1960s France, and others embraced hip-hop, house, techno, and Brazilian music. Tropicália, French ye-ye, Scottish indie bands, and whatever else could be found in the dustier corners of record stores became foundations for their songs. At their best, musicians found new ideas and perspective in forgotten LPs, and shared these gifts with a new set of listeners. Shibuya-kei intentionally moved in the opposite direction of the sleek pop of the day; if Komuro's productions were meant to be widely popular, Shibuya-kei intended to be cool for a niche audience.

While the halcyon days of Shibuya-kei were over by the new millennium, nostalgia still influenced younger acts. A small technopop revival sprouted from the Japanese underground, including the bands Motocompo and Polysics, who recalled the Devo/Plastics mode of jittery synthesized rock. Polysics even wore matching jumpsuits, a sartorial nod to Devo. A new wave of artists, dubbed neo-Shibuya-kei, exhibited Shibuya-kei's love of the sonic archive but with more electronic elements and faster tempos.

Although Nakata himself appears not to have listened to Pizzicato Five until the early 2000s,[10] Capsule slotted in comfortably with this new genre. The duo gave Parisian pop, bossa nova, and swing music a twenty-first-century update, and neo-Shibuya-kei acts like Hazel Nuts Chocolate and Sonic Coaster Pop guested on its albums. Nakata and Koshijima also became interested in fashion and visual aesthetics. The artwork for Capsule's albums and music videos recall the Continental vibe in Shibuya-kei, while Koshijima's dress in the video for Capsule's "Retro Memory" recalls the retro clothing of Pizzicato Five vocalist Maki Nomiya. Nakata was seeking his own voice within the style, and songs like the synthesizer-based dance track "Portable Airport," which sports a futuristic anime video that transports the protagonist to Paris, hinted at his future directions.

Nakata founded his own label Contemode, with Yamaha as its parent company and Avex Trax, the label for most of Komuro's artists, as distributor. Aside from a few artists like the band Copter4016882 and compilation albums of neo-Shibuya-kei artists, Contemode was a vessel for releases by Capsule and other Nakata-related projects, an investment in the producer and style by the recording industry. Contemode became a brand for Nakata and a new sound, its CDs sold in boutiques and its events were held at clubs across the city. While not mainstream, Nakata's music and image attracted the young and fashionable.

But what would ultimately guide Nakata to Perfume was not Capsule or Contemode, but Sync⇔Sync, his project with classmate Kinoko. While Nakata's work with Capsule borrowed heavily from Shibuya-kei, Sync⇔Sync was more electronically based, resulting in music that sounded crisper and more metallic. As these were school projects, Nakata and Kinoko, who wrote the lyrics and sang, may have allowed themselves to experiment with a larger array of sounds than they may have with a commercial release.

Nakata shared snippets of four Sync⇔Sync songs on his personal website, where someone associated with a fledgling, indie idol trio discovered them and found possible seeds for a new identity for his charges. As Nakata recalled about his first meeting with that team, "I thought they were really show-biz people, in a bad way. . . . I didn't like that kind of people. I didn't like the atmosphere. They weren't creative people."[11] But Nakata and Kinoko went along and were soon hired to produce songs for a group called Perfume.

3 A New Scent

Actor's School Hiroshima opened in 1999, in the downtown section of the western Japanese city. Established as part of local broadcasting company Television Shin-Hiroshima (TSS, an affiliate of the Fuji Television network), it was envisioned as a way to foster local talent and attract more attention to the region. Among the first class of students entering the school were Nishiwaki Ayaka, Kashino Yuka, and Ōmoto Ayano. All three traced their roots back to the Hiroshima region. Nishiwaki went to school in a mountainous region north of the city center, where bear sightings were not uncommon. Ōmoto hailed from Fukuyama, a castle city to the east of Hiroshima, while Kashino's family settled down in Hiroshima after moving around the country. All three were deeply inspired by the pop quartet Speed, and entered Actor's School Hiroshima hoping to improve their singing and dancing skills.[1] Nishiwaki and Kashino were slotted into the beginner-level courses, while Ōmoto's vocal skills earned her a spot in the advanced track.[2]

Within the school, students formed their own performance groups, focused on dancing and vocal training, with friends outside of classes. In early 2000, Nishiwaki and Kashino formed Perfume with another pupil named Kawashima Yūka; they had hoped to be a quartet, like Speed, but the fourth person had already committed to another group. As the three had the kanji character for fragrance in their names, the name "Perfume" (initially spelled in the phonetic hiragana alphabet) made sense. Meanwhile, Ōmoto was in a group called Happy Baby.[3]

These groups would perform at local dance competitions, such as the 2000 installment of the Japan Dance Delight contest held in the downtown music venue Chinatown. Aired on local access TV, the original Perfume introduced themselves awkwardly, like the camera-shy preteens they were, then performed a clap-heavy dance set to a hip-hop beat with samples of James Brown, fitting for a street-style competition. They received polite applause.

Thanks to the school's ties with TSS, the original Perfume performed on other occasions on local TV and introduced singing into its act. The three girls were fans of the recently released song "Super Jet Shoes," performed by local bubble-gum-popster Peachy, and they added the string-heavy number into the act. At the end of the year, Kawashima decided to leave Perfume—and the Actor's School entirely—in order to focus on her studies. Nishiwaki and Kashino decided to find a replacement for Kawashima (in part thanks to advice from Nishiwaki's mother, who thought a group featuring only two people lacked power).[4] Meanwhile, Ōmoto had become known as one of the better students at the Actor's School. In 2001, Nishiwaki asked her to join the group, and she agreed, finalizing the lineup for Perfume. Although Ōmoto's name did not include the character for fragrance, the group kept its name.

Perfume slowly gelled as the girls became closer friends and appeared on more local entertainment programs. The girls covered "Trouble" by the British duo Shampoo, while at local festivals they danced to a wide range of backing tracks, from bouncy J-pop to hip-hop. In one show, they showed off their own choreography to an unedited version of Lil' Kim's "How Many Licks?" with the moans still in. In 2002, Papparaa Kawai, formerly of popular 1980s rock band Bakufū Slump, wrote and produced the song "Omajinai perori" as Perfume's debut single on Momiji, the indie label run by Actor's School Hiroshima, for distribution within Hiroshima. It came from an entirely different sonic universe from the electropop that would gain them nationwide popularity later in the decade. The three sing chirpily, with the rough edges and cracked notes left without any benefit of electronic manipulation. The music is simple, with a chintzy drum machine beat and a synthesizer's skank accompanying an upbeat major-scale melody. The video is also simple, with the trio wearing schoolgirl uniforms and dancing like cheerleaders around an empty classroom. In a jarring transition, they are next whipping a creamy dessert and eating strawberries in midriff-baring Santa outfits—unseasonal for a March release.

At this point in time, Perfume was not aiming to become nationwide stars. "Omajinai perori" was a Hiroshima-only release, a single at the low price of ¥500 (about five dollars). The school-centric video and cutesy song aimed to establish them as idols, a type of J-pop performer that carries a specific set of expectations.

Idol Fancy

Like technopop, "idol" is a vague term. Similar to most mainstream-pop stars, these entertainers release songs, appear on TV, grace magazine covers, and so on, yet their relationship to their fan base calls for this additional tag. Although there is no shortage of male idols, the classic image of the idol is that of a young woman embarking on a journey. She is far from a polished performer at the outset, missing a note here and botching choreography there. She acts childish; the eternal icon Matsuda Seiko "took faltering steps and blushed, cried, and giggled for the camera."[5] This imperfection makes her more *kawaii* (cute) to her fans, who are encouraged to support them by joining fan clubs, cheering her in teams at performances, meeting her at meet-and-greet events, and buying records.[6] As supporters join idols on her musical journey, she amasses an extremely devoted fan base. That connection—between listener and idol—is especially important, and the building and maintaining of intimacy is central to the genre,[7] even if both sides recognize that the relationship is imagined.

The roots of idol pop owe something to France, although many Japanese women emerged as celebrated entertainers in the post–Second World War era. The singer Misora Hibari towered over the entertainment landscape in the 1950s and 1960s, and the twin-sister duo The Peanuts sang songs and starred in movies (e.g., as miniature fairies in *Mothra*). The idea of "idol" seems to have emerged from the French comedy film *Cherchez l'idole* (Look for the Idol, 1963), starring the Parisian singer Sylvie Vartan.[8] Her recording of the title theme for the film was the third best-selling single in Japan in 1965, edged out only by a pair of songs from American surf-rock band The Ventures.[9] Vartan came to Japan on a tour and starred in commercials. She was young, cute, and cool, and she appealed to the nation's youth. The term "idol" reflected all of those traits, and it appeared in magazines and movie taglines over the next few years.[10]

Japan's own idol scene blossomed thanks to TV talent shows like *Staa Tanjō* (A Star is Born, 1971–83), in which aspiring singers, many of them young girls, would compete against other contestants on this high-profile stage. In 1972, the program aired a pivotal moment in Japanese pop history. Three junior high school girls— Mori Masako, Sakurada Junko, and most notably, Yamaguchi Momoe—performed very well and were grouped into a unit dubbed Hana no Chūsan Torio (The Lovely Trio of Third-Year Junior High School Students). Playing to their schoolgirl image, they dressed in sailor uniforms. As they matured into successful solo careers, dozens of teenage idols took their place.[11]

Yamaguchi, the biggest star in the 1970s, set the model for idol music by embracing the characteristics of a "life-sized adolescent," which Aoyagi Hiroshi identifies as key to the style.[12] When her first single, "Toshigoro" (Coming of Age), proved disappointing, her management company, Horipro, decided on a risky tactic. Her second single, "Aoi kajitsu" (Unripe Fruit, 1973), opened with the lyrics, "You can do whatever you want with me." The suggestive lyrics (and the incongruity of having an innocent-looking fourteen-year-old sing them) made her stand out. A string of similar songs followed, including "Hito natsu no keiken" (An Experience One Summer, 1974), which had the line, "I'll give you a girl's most precious thing." These songs made her a superstar who also starred in sixteen movies, most of them with her future husband-to-be Miura Tomokazu, and fifteen television dramas over a scant seven years. Upon her marriage to Miura at the age of twenty-one, Yamaguchi retired from singing and acting. She set a template for Japanese idols that was picked up in the 1980s, when Matsuda Seiko ushered in a golden age of idol music,[13] charting what was then a record for number-one singles (25) and number-one albums (16).[14]

Popular idols were not confined to soloists; several idol groups were also noteworthy. The trio Candies, three school friends who debuted in 1972, was one of the decade's biggest groups, propelled forward by brass-heavy instrumentation and choreography that mimed the lyrics. The disco-leaning duo Pink Lady, who achieved even more sales success, became spokespersons for products as well as TV stars (including the short-lived American variety show *Pink Lady and Jeff*). Like the Candies, they danced in mirror fashion.

Idols also played with technopop (or more accurately, techno-kayō). Idol pop typically incorporates other current styles (such as disco in the case of Pink Lady), and the emergence of technopop coincided with the growth of idols in the late 1970s. One techno-idol crossover hit was Sakakibara Ikue's "Robot" (1980), an uptempo synthesizer-driven number whose lyrics, written by former Happy End drummer Matsumoto Takashi, spoke of a woman-robot ready to come to her lover. The members of YMO also produced songs for Japanese idols. In 1981, Pink Lady recruited YMO drummer Takahashi Yukihiro to work on the single "Last Pretender," a song that he had written the previous year for the singer Rajie and refitted with new lyrics. By then, the duo's popularity had fallen dramatically, and they hoped to find a different sound for a potential comeback. Co-written with Itoi Shigesato (of the video game *Earthbound*), "Last Pretender" sold poorly compared to Pink Lady's previous singles. Nonetheless, Takahashi later created numbers for Itō Tsukasa and Takai Mamiko, a member of the popular idol group, Onyanko Club.

Takahashi's bandmate Hosono Haruomi was more active in connecting idols with technopop. Although the songs he wrote for Matsuda Seiko (e.g., "Pink Mozart," 1984) featured string sections and guitar interludes above synthesizers, many of his contributions included electronic flourishes, his own personal insignia on the idol landscape. His tracks for former Candies' member Fujimura Miki feature technopop grooves underlining her airy vocals, and he gave Manabe Chiemi's 1982 debut album a sci-fi vibe with its synthesizers and

Kraftwerk-like percussion. He also worked for a brief time with the idol trio Starbow, who boasted a vague futuristic image (with costumes like Peter Pan) and danced in perfect unison with one another.

As the heyday of idol music in the 1980s made way for J-pop in the 1990s, the market shifted in favor of more polished singers such as Amuro Namie and UA. Groups like Amuro's original outfit, Super Monkeys, even avoided the classification of idol. But in 1998, an updated, cooler-sounding kind of idol hit the airwaves with Morning Musume's first single, "Morning Coffee." A medium-tempo song in an acoustic-guitar accompaniment, it sounded as if it could be performed by a singer-songwriter or indie-pop band, but was in fact sung in interlocking fashion by the five young women. The group's cute image tapped into a nostalgia for the golden age of idols in the 1980s, sometimes taking it into ironic territory.[15] The group soon expanded in size, moving toward the idol model laid out in the mid-1980s by Onyanko Club, in which a large lineup of female members continually changes as members "graduate" from the group and are replaced by younger members.

Morning Musume were at peak popularity nationwide when the members of Perfume entered the Actor's School Hiroshima. The echoes of idol music can be heard in those awkward notes and plain-spoken lyrics in "Omajinai perori."

Tokyo Girls

By the time that Perfume released their second Hiroshima-area single, "Kareshi boshūchū" (Boyfriend Wanted), the group had firmly established themselves as local idols. The girls appeared occasionally on TSS, popping up on local morning shows, and danced at local festivals. Once again crafted by Papparaa Kawai, "Kareshi boshūchū" opens with a semi-joking, *enka*-style passage, in which the girls take turns lamenting their single status, while a baritone yelps in the background like a bulldog. The song then bursts into a steel-drum tropical hop, describing the qualities they would want in a potential boyfriend. For fans of the post-Nakata Perfume, it is jarring to listen, from the girls' channeling *enka* to the super silly atmosphere building up to the la-la chorus. The song sounds like a joke, but it is also designed for the girls' high-pitched voices. It seems the polar opposite of Perfume after Nakata Yasutaka joined the fold.

As goofy and atypical as the song sounded, it hinted at a higher potential for the trio. In 2002, Perfume met Mizuno Mikiko, a choreographer and dance teacher who would later play an important role in shaping their signature dance style. After graduating from the Actor's School in 2003, Perfume signed with Amuse and moved to Tokyo. There, they took part in the Bee-Hive, a special project whereby seventeen of Amuse's female performers lived in a dorm in southwest Tokyo. A web camera, called the Bee-Hive Camera, was installed in the basement, and the resident performers talked to the device at various times. In theory, they would be speaking to the hardcore fans willing to tune in to the live stream. This approach was ahead of its time—no shortage of J-pop acts, idol or otherwise, would use similar concepts in the coming years—but its use was a bit strange. The members of Perfume treat the camera as a place for random thoughts, as when A-chan talks about how her bangs are growing, or performance art of sorts, as when Nocchi interacts with a stuffed doll in the shape of Disney's Piglet.

The arrival of Nakata Yasutaka and Kinoko Emi onto Perfume's team in 2003 marked a new period of development for the group as it searched for a new unique sound. The pair moved fast to compose songs, with Kinoko writing lyrics and Nakata producing the sound itself. Perfume's first single on the indie imprint Bee-Hive, "Sweet Donuts," was released in August 2003.

In a series of featured articles in *Music Magazine* published a few months after the release of *Game*, Yoshida Gō referred to "Sweet Donuts" as "so perfect, both as idol pop or as technopop."[16] The arpeggios (skipped notes) of high-pitched synthesizers and fast beat recalled the music and vibe of technopop of the late 1970s, and this retro aspect connected Perfume to the sound of Shibuya-kei. There was also an electronic sound resembling a laser—one of Nakata's favorite sounds at the time, also heard in Capsule's "Portable Airport." As an idol song, the lyrics are less about donuts than they are about heartbreak, a running theme in Kinoko's writing. The song opens, "Your last word suddenly became cold and left a bruise in my heart."[17] The bleepy music and Perfume's chipper delivery mask the hurt underneath.

More sonically telling was the B-side, a cover of 1980s band Juicy Fruit's "Jenny wa gokigen naname" (Jenny's in a Bad Mood). One of techno-kayō's biggest singles, the original band had merged synth notes and monotone vocal delivery with guitars and drums. Perfume's version was done at a faster tempo and with an overload of electronics, making it sound comical, like someone manning an oversized control panel. To have Perfume tackle this song was itself a statement, as not only was "Jenny" a most successful technopop-style song, but Juicy Fruits was also known for their adeptness in transforming synthesizer-heavy sounds into crowd-pleasing pop.

Indeed, Nakata's investment in past styles carried over into Perfume's next two singles. "Monochrome Effect," a peppy, danceable melody, featured a video with black-and-white, retro-dress segments that would have been at home in a Flipper's Guitar clip. Still, their third single, "Vitamin Drop" (2004), introduced a critical idea that would come to define the group's sound. The song exaggerates Nakata's retro feel, so that it actually sounds like a jingle for health supplements (although the lyrics dwelled on the sour side of love, such as "verbal abuse").[18] Nakata's production was becoming more intricate in the use of electronic sounds; most strikingly, he played with the vocals. In previous productions, they sound untouched, and all the imperfections came through loud and clear, as with many other idols. On "Vitamin Drop," Nakata smooths them out, adding a faint electronic hum to their syllables. He synchronizes their voices so that they sing together, and their voices blend with the other instruments in the mix. "Vitamin Drop" hinted at the strides Perfume would soon make.

A Different Track

With their technopop sound and somewhat dark lyrics, Perfume's singles of 2003 and 2004 did not sound like typical idol songs, which replicated the cheery pop of Morning Musume. Its management noticed and briefly reoriented Perfume as traditional idols. Akihabara, the Tokyo district of electronic stores (many of them specializing in 1970s-era goods) and all things idol, became Perfume's focus for a year. The three members handed out flyers to pedestrians and performed shows in cramped parking lots, in an effort to spread its name.

They teamed up with Momoi Haruko, an anime voice actor and singer/songwriter, to record a song called "Akihabalove."

Produced by Momoi, the track has more in common with the Eurobeat-inspired rumblers on which Komuro Tetsuya built his name in the 1990s than the 1980s technopop that Nakata references. "Akhihabalove" also featured some dramatic, over-the-top moments, with Perfume showing the full range of their voices; they overshadowed the monotone delivery of Nakata's songs. The fast-paced song was also suitable for any idol group.

"Akihabalove" did not transform Perfume into a charting phenomenon. It did leave many with the impression that Perfume was just another Akihabara-based unit, an image that would stick with it for the next two years. Perfume would soon find a way to shake off that label, as well as that of traditional idols. But first, a few more trials awaited.

4   Brave New World

Polite applause met the members of Perfume as they walked down the spiral stairs leading up to the Genius Bar. The group were preparing to start a special four-song performance for a sparse crowd at the Apple Store—more accurately, the front-right corner of the Apple Store—in downtown Osaka on August 19, 2006. "We hope you at least remember our name by the end of the show," A-chan said in her modest introduction.[1] Perfume danced in front of a computer screen, the sleek white plastic and digital graphics behind them an appropriate backdrop for the electropop. The crowd—a little over a dozen people total—bobbed along to the music, while customers coming in and out of the busy store walked right in front of them as if they were another display stand.

The trio was promoting the just-released *Perfume ~ Complete Best ~*, a compilation of all of its singles and most B-sides to date. Yet despite the best-of pretention in the name, the group was yet to achieve any real sales success. Its best-selling single at that point, "Computer City," had sold 4,000 copies and peaked at #45 on the Oricon charts. To their supporters, *Complete Best* inspired more fear than optimism. As Kashiyuka recalled on their radio show, *Perfume Locks,* in 2010, "At that time, a rumor had spread among our fans that we were going to disband. . . . When we held handshake events, many people would ask us that question or mention it. Like, 'please don't break up!'"[2] *Complete Best* felt more like a parting gift for fans than a celebration, gathering up then out-of-print singles in one place from a pop unit that had seemingly gone as far as it could.

Electro Image

The previous year, Perfume had moved to the major imprint Tokuma Japan Communications. In an odd exchange, one member of Tokuma management communicated what could be read as fatherly caution, realism, or a cutdown to spur the women on. When the trio visited the company's head office in Tokyo to introduce themselves, a senior executive told them the company would let them release three CD singles. "So take that as a good memory, and maybe you should think about other careers."[3] The teenagers were shocked to hear these words when they were putting all their energies into the group and were feeling excited about recording for a major label. But just in case, the trio enrolled in local colleges.

Tokuma altered Perfume's image from their cute look, full of bright colors, typical of Japanese idols to a sci-fi look, with post-*Matrix* black dresses with one leather glove, and videos incorporating computer-generated graphics and flying-orb robots. The cheery, 1960s space-age vibe of Perfume's videos was updated to the stark, black-and-white Digitalism that 2006 audiences might have imagined the near future to look like. While Nakata was not involved in the visual side of Perfume's presentation, he told the magazine *Quick Japan* that his sound, which he refused to define to management, helped to shape it. As he speculates, the management thought his music sounded like video games, so they adopted the technocratic angle.[4]

The music was also changing. The group's major-label debut single, "Linear Motor Girl" (September 2005), did not stray far from the combination of Shibuya-kei and golden-age technopop that had defined Nakata's style. Its zippy tempo and 8-bit burbles would fit well into a Japanese pico-pop (technopop) compilation. The most pronounced change is the song's topic, with a heavier emphasis on technology (linear motors), while Kinoko moved away from the heavier side of romance to simply capturing the feelings of falling in love. Nakata's manipulation of Perfume's voices is also more audible, particularly in the autotune timbres of the chorus. Fitting for a song evoking movement, the music slows (around 0:27) and starts again (0:33), shooting forward like a hovertrain from a future era. The song gives the listener warning right before settling into a nice groove, a digitized voice asks, "Are you ready?" before a string of 8-bit sounds ushers the song forward.

Nakata also incorporated new sounds that would become central to Perfume's success. Some of these sounds had first surfaced in Capsule, whose *L.D.K. Lounge Designers Killer* (2005), released in the same month as Perfume's single, featured harder-hitting bass lines, more aggressive beats, and distorted computer sounds. It showed the influence of European electronic artists such as Underworld, Justice, and in particular, Daft Punk. The French duo had recently released their third album, *Human After All,* a pounding and feedback-heavy work in which the pair viewed technology in dystopian terms, frequently invoking Orwell ("Television Rules the Nation"). Daft Punk member Thomas Bangalter said the album was not intended to make the listener feel good.[5]

While Nakata was not referencing *1984*, the heavier sonic elements and the technological references on the Daft Punk album were becoming more evident in his work. After nearly half a decade spent playing in Shibuya-kei, Capsule's 2006 album *Fruit's Clipper* marked the moment when Nakata took on a new direction toward heavily processed club sounds and came into his own as a producer. He mentioned in an interview that Capsule's initial sound was for women, and he now wanted to make something more appealing to men.[6] In another, he said,

> Thinking of people inside their homes surrounded by fashionable interiors and totally immersed in themselves made me feel sort of disgusted. . . . I wanted to make it so that even if your surroundings were really loud, it'd become part of the music as you listened to it on headphones using an iPod or a Walkman. That's the concept this time. Something that sounds cool amid the noise.[7]

The influence of *Human After All* comes through in the use of quick-fire, electronically generated words; when Capsule sings, "earl-gray drinking harmony croquis crisis many money break-it" in "Fruit's Clipper," it echoes Daft Punk's "Buy it, use it, break it, fix it, trash it, change it, mail, upgrade it" in "Technologic." The song "Robot Disco" also boasts a similar conceit to the French duo's "Robot Rock." But after the series of computerized gibberish in "Fruits Clipper," Koshijima Toshiko's voice rises up and delivers a sweet passage, punctuated by a sunny guitar line. Although owing much to the pummeling nature of *Human After All*, songs such as "Jelly" and "Dreamin' Dreamin'" highlighted warmth without sacrificing a club-worthy thump.

Nakata's new aesthetic carried over to Perfume's next singles, "Computer City" (January 2006) and "Electro World"

(June 2006). Kinoko had left the Perfume project, giving Nakata complete control of Perfume's music and lyrics. Along with "Linear Motor Girl," "Computer City" and "Electro World" have been dubbed the "near-future trilogy" by fans, thanks to their heavy electropop sound and lyrics centered on a digital setting. Whereas "Linear Motor Girl" zoomed toward utopia, the chugging "Computer City" meditated on the then-blossoming age of information. A club-ready beat and electronically manipulated singing propelled the song forward and earned positive reviews from Japanese music journalists. The protagonist at the center of "Computer City" complains of the confines of a town "made from perfect calculation"—that is, fake and confining—and dreams of escape with her love, "the only thing that's not fake."[8]

If "Computer City" presented an unsure view of a technologically centered place, "Electro World" sounded downright apocalyptic. It introduced harsher electropop tones to Perfume's style, featuring more heavily processed singing and an electric guitar adding tension to the synthesizer lines, although the hook remained pop-friendly. It is a thematic rarity in the group's catalog, "Electro World" is *sad*, both on a lyrical level and in how it sounds, with Nakata's fill-every-space approach sounding suffocating and downtrodden. The version that would eventually appear on *Perfume ~ Complete Best ~* prefaces the main song with a brief ambient passage, the loneliest-sounding few seconds of any Perfume song. But lines such as "Everything I can see / Everything I can touch, too / Has no reality," and "Who flipped the switch on for this world? / Soon it will be no more"[9] do not imagine the fascist possibilities that intrigued Daft Punk, as much as observe the fleeting nature of contemporary technological wonders.

Fan Service

These first three major-label singles marked the digital transformation of Perfume, but still sold poorly—"Computer City" entered the Oricon top 50 with a measly 4,000 units moved, then a career best. The J-pop landscape in 2006 was dominated by boy bands from the Johnny's agency (e.g., Kat-tun, SMAP) and female pop vocalists like Kōda Kumi and Hamasaki Ayumi, who wrote their own lyrics and projected strong personalities and fashion sense. Electropop, to the extent that Perfume was incorporating, was out of the mainstream. Idol music was hibernating, the peak commercial days of Morning Musume over. The times did not seem welcoming for Perfume.

But Perfume went on, sometimes introducing themselves as a "technopop unit," dancing to music by Digitalism at live shows that remained intimate affairs. Their own variety TV show, "Pa Pa Pa Pa Pa Pa Perfume," aired on an obscure cable channel called Enta!371, and mostly featured live footage of the band (to small crowds) and a few silly segments (Perfume visits—a music magazine!).

On Valentine's Day 2007, the trio released "Fan Service," a single to reassure fans they were not dissolving. With a DVD and twenty-page book packaged like a Valentine's treat, the single looked like a gift to fans. It debuted at 33rd on the Oricon chart, the group's highest yet, but overall sales still remained low. But the first song "Chocolate Disco" would not be obscure for long.

In keeping with its drop date, the words to "Chocolate Disco" focus on the Japanese tradition of women giving men chocolates on Valentine's Day. The central conceit is that a classroom looks like a dance floor on February 14: "Girls are calculating about their plan / Boys are expecting something / Girls flutter in expectation and joy / Boys pretend not to care about it."[10] The music (discussed further in the next chapter) was the most outright poppy they had sounded since jumping to a major label, but free of the idol awkwardness of their indie days. And at the center of it was a simple but catchy hook, the sort of chorus built for group shout-alongs in a karaoke box.

Pop star Kimura Kaela listened to "Chocolate Disco" and was smitten. Kimura was at the peak of her popularity, as her recently released third album, *Scratch,* had topped the Oricon charts, going on to sell over 300,000 copies. It is not clear how she first heard the song: Kimura herself said she saw the music video while out and about in Tokyo, and checked out more Perfume clips and songs soon after.[11] However, Perfume recalled in a 2010 radio show that they and Kimura employed the same event promoter, who gave her the trio's music, although she had not responded until 2007.[12] What is not in dispute is that Kimura exposed "Chocolate Disco" to a massive new audience on the March 27, 2007 edition of the radio program, *Oh! My Radio*, which was aired on popular Tokyo radio station J-Wave. "Their music is something you rarely hear nowadays. It sounds kind of long forgotten," Kimura said on the show. "I really hope they make a big leap forward."[13] She then played "Chocolate Disco," and continued to play it and other Perfume songs over the course of the next four weeks. Her seal of approval helped sell mainstream listeners on a group whose music, as she noted, sounded totally different from the sounds then dominating the J-pop landscape, including Kimura's own punk-pop tinged cuts.

Plastic Fantastic

One of those tuning into Kimura's show was Akira Tomotsugi, a commercial director working with the Japan Advertising

Council, a non-profit organization creating public service announcements. After hearing "Chocolate Disco," he decided to have Perfume star in an upcoming advertisement meant to promote recycling.[14] A new song would need to be written, to serve as a soundtrack for a spot encouraging people to separate papers and plastics. Many J-pop singles start in this way—a company wants a song for an upcoming advertising campaign, so they approach an artist they have in mind to make it. As previously mentioned, YMO's "Behind the Mask" was initially created for a watch commercial.

In the thirty-second clip, Perfume are center stage in synchronized robo-style dancing, surrounded by actors, covered in plastic bottles or shrubbery, expressing annoyance at the litter around them. By the end of the clip, the performers have learned how to separate recyclable trash as Perfume keep on dancing. The spot aired on the national broadcast channel NHK, introducing the group to a nationwide audience. As television remains the key by which a song becomes a hit, or a local pop unit becomes nationwide stars, this commercial was Perfume's breakout moment. A public service announcement about proper garbage disposal might not have been the coolest introduction, but just gracing the airwaves was all that Perfume needed.

Just as important was the song Nakata produced for the advertisement—"Polyrhythm," which would become the opening track on *Game*. This track was his first time writing music for media that would be heard by hundreds of thousands of new listeners. In his early years living in Tokyo, he had scored a small-time film, but the stakes here were much higher. Initially, Nakata planned a literal interpretation of his client's campaign—he imagined having Perfume sing the word "recycle" a bunch over the course of the song, to underline the point of the commercial. People advised him that he did not need to do *that* much to please the Ad Council.[15] Rather, Nakata chose to follow his muses, with the only nod to the commercial hiding in the title—the "poly" doubles as a subtle reference to polyethylene terephthalate, the material that makes up most plastic bottles in Japan. What could have been a forgettable novelty jingle about properly disposing plastics became a song that could stand all on its own (discussed in Chapter 5).

Upward Bound

Perfume was now on a roll, and its opportunities snowballed through the rest of 2007. A set of solo shows at Tokyo's Daikanyama Unit in May sold out, and Perfume was invited to perform at that August's Summer Sonic, one of Japan's biggest annual summer rock festivals; the group played the Dance Stage, in recognition of its electropop sound that it was exposing to a wide audience. Its media exposure ratcheted up, appearing on various TV and radio programs (including Kimura's show). The official breakthrough came in September, when the single "Polyrhythm" moved 17,000 units in its first week, landing Perfume in the Oricon top-10 singles chart for the first time, at number seven (it would go on to sell a total of 77,000 copies).[16] The next single—"Baby Cruising Love" with "Macaroni" on the back—debuted in the top three.

Momentum started to build for the group, and all-important TV coverage came next. In addition to commercials for bite-size ice cream treats and computer software, Perfume was invited to popular morning shows and variety programs. The women were shown heading to famous Hiroshima-style okonomiyaki restaurants for a cooking lesson, or making a triumphant appearance on a hometown talk show—an embarrassed "Ahhhh!" was all the members could muster when footage of their local-idol days appeared on screen. They were getting a lot of attention.

In two years, Perfume had gone from sideshows at the Apple Store to Summer Sonic, success-against-all-odds story that pop idol managers could only dream of. Still, plenty of artists experienced a rush of popularity only to fade from view shortly afterward. Perfume needed something to establish themselves and their burbling dance-pop sound firmly in the Japanese music landscape. That came one year later, with *Game*.

5 Play the Game

Although talk about Perfume centers on its near-future image and sound, including the robot-like voices of its three singers, one of the first sounds one hears on *Game* is a person taking a breath. This small but vital detail epitomizes the feel of the album: for all its digital trappings, *Game* is about human emotion, as the tracks demonstrate.

Perfume's debut album begins with "Polyrhythm"—the song that catapulted the group to the mainstream and was the introduction to Perfume's music for many listeners. Its four minutes contain everything that makes *Game* a memorable listening experience. "Polyrhythm" sounded completely different from anything happening in J-pop or anywhere else when it came out in 2007. The label also noticed and tried to change it, while Nakata fought hard for it to remain in its boundary-pushing state.

The thirty-second commercial features only the chorus, the catchiest part of the song; the final version builds up to it. After that initial inhale, A-chan starts singing, her voice sounding clear with a distinct electronic buzz. When Kashiyuka takes over a few seconds later, and Nocchi just after that, it is hard to notice the changeover, as they sound like the same singer, ever so slightly manipulated digitally. The hook is just as ear-catching as in the commercial, all three joining together to sing over a beat punctuated by an octave-oscillating bass and a four-to-the-floor drum beat. Airy swooshes divide sections of the song.

Had Nakata stopped here, he would have already had himself a solid pop song, highlighting the electropop edge and manipulated vocals. But Nakata went for something extra and different. Around the time he started working on the commercial, Nakata developed an interest in polyrhythms, two or more rhythmical patterns playing at the same time and sometimes conflicting with one another. As mentioned previously, "Polyrhythm" contained a reference to the material used to make plastic bottles, the sort of detail sure to delight an ad representative's face. Nakata also exploited its literal definition.

At the end of the chorus, the music does not go on to the next verse, as we might expect. Instead, a coda to the chorus lets polyrhythms take over: the trio sings repeating loops of "polyrhythm" (or the Japanese pronunciation, po-ri-ri-zu-mu), then "rhythm" (ri-zu-mu), and "polyloop" (po-ri-ru-u-pu). These loops of five, three, and five syllables are overlaid against a four-beat meter, so that the listener hears the syllables emphasizing different beats of a four-beat measure. The first "po" on "polyrhythm," which we expect to hear on a strong beat, lands first on beat 1, then on 3, and then on 2, then on 4, and then on 3, and so forth. These rotating emphases make the listener feel as if she were spinning around and around, polylooping in polyrhythm. The recurring Japanese lyric, *kurikaesu*, means "to repeat," also reflecting this action. The song then snaps back to the second verse, building up to another shiny-sounding chorus and ends with another polyrhythmic section.

Nothing on the Oricon charts sounded anything like this coda to the chorus. The closest comparisons were more experimental Japanese groups, such as Rovo and Date Course Pentagon Royal Garden, rather than more comparable charters like Utada Hikaru or Hamasaki Ayumi. Tokuma Japan wanted this polyrhythmic section cut out of the song entirely because its unusual nature might estrange J-pop listeners.[1] But Nakata recognized that he had something special with "Polyrhythm." Up to this point, the producer had been content to concentrate on creating music for Perfume, without worrying about costumes, music videos, promotion, and other show-business necessities; the trio handled this job well. For "Polyrhythm," he did something he had seemingly never done before—he fought for his creation to go unchanged, for the titular section to stay on the album.[2]

He won. Tokuma Japan allowed the coda to stay on the album version; as a concession to the label, it affixed an "Extra Short Edit" to the single release.[3] But the listeners first heard the original version of "Polyrhythm," with the unorthodox rhythm intact. Nakata thus defined how the group would sound. And "Polyrhythm" catapulted Perfume into the mainstream, with that very section being the unique highlight that captured people's attention. Even in that moment when the human voice gets turned into a machine-like loop, the song sounds warm, inviting, and sweet, like a voice trying to find stability as it keeps stuttering. This human gesture, along with the computerized sound and innovative rhythmical play, epitomizes Perfume's boundary-pushing sounds at the time.

Controlling the Track

Nakata's role with Perfume was unique for a J-pop group in the 2000s. As Nakata told Quick Japan, "Yeah, I'm not producing them totally, so that's the biggest difference between Perfume and Capsule"; that is, he did not concern himself with Perfume's artistic direction or style, as he did for Capsule.[4] He also

Play the Game

51

maintained a distance from the three members themselves; he only saw them live for the first time at the end of 2007, four years after starting to work with them. He simply handled the music, and after Kinoko left, the lyrics, without much interference from the label or group. He had the control and freedom to experiment with Perfume's sound. Most producers working with a pop group do not get this luxury.

Nakata's approach to making a song also went against the traditional J-pop grain. Normally, the songwriter records a demo and puts together the supporting instrumentation, and the vocals are recorded on top of it. According to Nakata, this method simply did not work for Perfume. Instead, he wrote the melody and lyrics, and then had the trio record their vocals as quickly as possible. By 2007, personal home recording software had reached such a level that Nakata could create all of *Game* in his private studio. There, he recorded vocals, with his singers sitting down into a small closet-like space. Rather than singing passionately, they were encouraged to sing as if they are speaking. Such instructions frustrated the three singers, who had been trained since Actor's School to sing dramatically and expressively. Nakata also played with the qualities of each singer's voice, changing A-chan's strong vocal style to softer one and emphasizing the softness of Kashiyuka voice and the clarity of Nocchi's voice.[5] Kashiyuka recalled that throughout the making *Game*, at least one of the members was crying in frustration.[6] This method resulted in their voices sounding flatter, making them easier to manipulate and blend with the background track. Nakata then tinkered with these vocals, compressing and running them through autotune and other tools. Such a process may have been more difficult at a rented studio, where other managers' expectations would hover over him, not to mention time limits. As Nakata said in a TV program, sitting in his home studio, "I make songs in an environment where everything is in reach. . . . In other words, I don't do things that I cannot do in here." He compared the whole process to cooking food, matching different elements.[7]

Part of what makes Perfume's debut so endearing is that it is a catchy, danceable, front-to-back set of pop music. Like many J-pop albums, *Game* is a collection of potential singles rather than a holistic album that needs to be heard straight through, and it more than makes up for any lack of overall concept in tightly constructed individual tunes that command your attention. "Plastic Smile" bounces forward on a relentlessly cheerful synthesizer melody and rocking bass that recalls the synth-heavy pop of the 1980s. As hinted at on "Polyrhythm," *Game*'s most immediate moments come when a set of sonically pleasing syllables is milked—the "la la" introducing the flashbang high-step of "Secret Secret," the "la la la" backing "Twinkle Snow Powdery Snow," or the succulent "cho-ko-re-i-to dis'-ko!" spinning at the center of "Chocolate Disco." As with many great pop songs, the importance of lyrical meaning melts away when the words just sound good together, blending into the group's electrified sound.

Although many critics fixated on the group's near-future image and electropop sound—narratives played up by Perfume's management, to make them stand out—*Game* actually sports a variety of timbres, allowing it to be continually engaging. In "Baby Cruising Love," which was released as a single in advance of the album, the central instrument is the piano, it turns lyrical and rhythmic like 1980s pop star Akiko Yano's playing, with surprising jazz-inflected harmonies in the pre-chorus. Repeating patterns of synthesizers and xylophones interweave like the titular beings on "Butterfly," giving the disco-tinged number an atmosphere of statelessness. The strumming guitar of "Puppy Love" gives way to a celesta-like riff reminiscent of rock band Quruli's "Bara no hana."

An anomaly on *Game* is "Macaroni," which was originally included on the "Baby Cruising Love" single. The song unfolds at a much slower tempo (pace) than any other song on the album, and while the three women's voices still carry a computerized edge, they seem more front-mixed than in the rest of the album. After a hellacious opening five-song run featuring *Game*'s biggest singles ("Polyrhythm," "Chocolate Disco," "Baby Cruising Love"), "Macaroni" offers a breather before the second half blasts off, a pleasant stroll following a mad dash. But it also highlights Nakata's songwriting skill, with surprising vocal leaps and jazz-inflected harmonic changes, particularly in the chorus and bridge. At one point, the song suddenly stops in silence, emphasizing the words the women have just sung—cooking macaroni soup, holding hands, relishing being together with another—before moving on. Like many of Nakata's songs on *Game*, "Macaroni" holds some fine subtleties beneath its pop-song exterior.

A Different Type of Idol

The attention that Nakata paid to the music of Perfume was unusual for idols, where the music is usually considered secondary. As Nakata told Quick Japan, "For most other idols, the musicians don't put much effort into it. . . . They can get serious, but then people say, 'This music is too cool for an idol.'"[8] Indeed, "cool" is a word that Nakata frequently uses in interviews, dating before Perfume and well after *Game*. This fascination with cool partially explains why he switched Capsule's sound from cheery Shibuya-kei pop to harder-hitting electropop, and it always seems to lurk in the back of his mind as he creates. For Perfume, he needed to find the right balance between pop and cool. Before *Game*'s release, he told an interviewer, "Perfume could just be an idol group that sounds and looks like Capsule, and that would be the most boring thing ever."[9] The loud bass lines and robotic vocal sounds were fashionable for club devotees but hardly trendy in general Japanese mainstream culture. He consciously held back from using those elements.[10]

As previously mentioned, *Game* came out at a point where idol music was out of fashion. *Game* came out at the perfect moment, when Perfume could simply be considered J-pop. Had the group waited a year or two, it would have been eclipsed by AKB48, a music-business behemoth that restarted the idol boom that has dominated through the time of this writing. But when it was released, Perfume had no easy comparisons, leaving *Game* to be appreciated for its clever pop songs that enjoyed widespread appeal. A-chan, Nocchi, and Kashiyuka were also vital to *Game*'s success, connecting with fans in live performances and media appearances and pulling off more intricate and precise choreography than is usual for idols. *Game* offered clever pop songs with something for everyone.

Digital Love

Perfume could have embraced the technological image that their near-future trilogy had introduced, with each song mentioning some futuristic electronic item or dwelling on the consequences of a rapidly changing world. Doing so could also have branded them as a novelty, the girl group singing exclusively about the items you might find in a future electronics store. While Perfume held on to the high-tech vibe, as shown through the technological display in the group's videos and concerts, the lyrics shifted away from technology, as signaled "Chocolate Disco," about clumsy teenage interaction. *Game* made it clear that Perfume may *sound* like cutting-edge technology, but its themes will not be solely focused on it.

One song that does reference technology is the title track. The singer asks the addressee to "play the game," choosing which way his feelings will go, as if she were a mannequin or object in a video game. The buzz-saw-like, octave-oscillating bass, the distorted guitar, and skittering drums recall the constricting electropop of Daft Punk's *Human After All*. When the chorus plays—"Play the game / Try the new world"—it is surrounded by an overwhelming wall of electro noise. The lyrics seem apt for 2008, when social networking and smartphones were starting to grow in Japan, making technology look like an opener to new social worlds.

"Ceramic Girl" offers a technology-themed counterpoint to "Game." Unlike the protagonist beckoning her lover to play her in "Game," the singer here declares herself to be a "ceramic girl / it's a brave new world," who "would like to fall in love / but [my] antenna can't reach [you]." She says, "I want to live in the world, a world that seems transparent." The ceramic girl seems to refer to a technological creation—most likely a robot with ceramic covering, but perhaps also the piezoelectric ceramic components powering cellular phones, the object of obsessive attention of many a woman or man. The sound of the song also fully embraces technology: the synthesizers seem to sound more neon-bright and syncopated, while the bass sounds louder than in any other song on the album. Most notably, the three singer's voices seem most radically transformed on this song: in the instrumental bridge, their voices are cut up into individual notes, transforming them into another synthesizer part. Clearly the ceramic girl is artificial, yet she has human emotions: as she says, "I want to fall in love, so believe in my telepathic [message]," and as she declares, "[this feeling is the only] / un-manufactured thing," the instruments drop out to highlight her words. The lyrics to "Ceramic Girl" imply that human love transforms a mere technological object. A similar theme can be seen in the trio's videos for "Secret Secret," in which the three women are mannequins and are brought to life by eating Pino ice cream, and "Spring of Life" (2013), in which they are robots that come alive.

While voice manipulation techniques like autotune can sound robot-like, many artists use it as a timbral marker; for example, Cher's "Believe" (1998) and Kanye West's *808s and Heartbreak* (2008) may have robotic-sounding voices to an electronic beat, but the songs still express heartbreak. Similarly, *Game* uses futuristic sounds to address familiar activities and feelings. According to a 2008 interview in the magazine TV Bros., the fact that Nakata writes the melody before the lyrics does not preclude him from aiming for lyrical meaning.[11] The minimal lyrics of "Take Me Take Me" simply repeat the title and "take me tonight" in varying tones of intensity. This familiar setup in EDM, in which it is often delivered in lustful tones, seems strangely innocent in Perfume's high voices.

Indeed, love dominates Game on a thematic level, but the lyrics are not as relentless upbeat as the music might imply. When "Baby Cruising Love" was released as a single, Nakata envisioned it as a winter love song. Such songs, about a character alone during the colder months, reflecting sadly on a loss (of a love) but carrying on, is a trope in mainstream J-pop, and "Baby Cruising Love" fits this trope. Nakata uses the word "kōkai" (航海), meaning "voyage," which has a homonym (後悔) meaning "regret"; the first lines of verse could be heard either as "Isn't the fate of love . . . somewhat like the voyage of two people?" or "the regret of two people."[12] The plaintive longing expressed in the lyrics cuts through the bouncy setting and the autotuned singing. These are among the moments that makes *Game* such a compelling listen—when a feeling of uncertainty or melancholy sneaks into the poppy joyousness.

There are also details that color the affect of these songs. One of the most memorable moments in "Chocolate Disco," the album's sweet and upbeat cut, comes during the rebuilding of the beat before the coda; the beats cut out, and the hook is repeated most softly as synthesizer notes build texture behind it. It takes "Chocolate Disco" from bouncy happiness to nervous, building excitement, appropriate for a song about teens giving their crushes sweets. Most songs in *Game* feature something disrupting the pure, poppy joy of the songs. "Plastic Smile" sounds a little like throwback technopop, but the lyrics feel somewhat awry, with the music cutting out at "Something's come off." "Twinkle Snow Powdery Snow" sounds like chirpy fun in the winter, but its softer passages raise concerns that newfound love might be fleeting.

The sentiments explored across *Game* are universal and complex, to which anyone, including the three performers or the audience members, could relate. The album closer "Puppy Love" displays this duality well. The track sounds bubbly, but the lyrics focus on a character dealing with a *tsundere* type—someone who is usually aloof and rude, but becomes warm and affectionate when alone. This type of character is common in cartoons and anime, with Helga from *Hey Arnold* being one example. To some degree, "Puppy Love" is looking at a very sweet, childish type of love, the sort of cute relationship you might find at an elementary or junior high school. Yet the song is obsessed with that gap—does he like me, or not? The song does not reach any conclusion, happy or sad, which adds a bittersweet quality to this "Puppy Love."

The best description of Perfume's music came from a different performer working with Nakata, a few years after *Game*'s release. Kyary Pamyu Pamyu told *The Fader*, "Perfume always sounds like innocent girls who have fallen in love pure-heartedly with someone."[13] The emotional rush of that spark is present throughout *Game*, but so is all the uncertainty that follows. How does he feel about me? Can it last? Perfume's debut brought these timeless feelings to an electronic setting.

Looking Back at *Game*

Like the YMO and Juicy Fruits in the age of technopop, *Game* adjusts trendy styles for mainstream listeners. It marked the peak of a period in Nakata's career during which he experimented heavily with electropop, beginning with Capsule's *Fruits Clipper* and Perfume's first major album, which struck a balance between cutting-edge and radio-ready. As YMO and Komuro Tetsuya had done previously, Nakata created hits that added new stylistic twists to the popular music scene while retaining his own artistry.

The members of Perfume consolidated their newly formed identity upon the album's release. A frequent complaint leveled at *Game* (and much of Perfume's music) is that it lacks "character," implying that Nakata's heavy compression of vocals erases the vocalists' personal quirks that make them unique. While Nakata himself says that he aims to keep the three voices at similar timbres, such remarks downplay the emotional complexity of *Game*. It owns its place among the best J-pop albums. It also allowed A-chan, Nocchi, and Kashiyuka to shine in TV appearances and live shows, proving them to be charismatic and charming; they really do excel at being idols. Perfume were confirmed as superstars, changing the face of Japanese popular music in the digital age.

6 Take Off

Game proved to be a massive success. The album topped the Oricon album charts in the week of its release, outselling new albums from rock band HY and folk duo Yuzu—outfits that had been far more in tune with dominant J-pop trends in recent years, with number-one spots on the charts; it also topped Mariah Carey's latest album. Perfume's first original album held its position in the top ten for five weeks, and by the end of 2008, *Game* had sold more than 390,000 copies, making it the twenty-third best-selling album of the year.[1] It was a stunning leap for a group that had barely touched the outer edges of the rankings before "Polyrhythm."

Japanese media outlets placed *Game* in a larger historical context. Oricon celebrated the "brilliant achievement" of Perfume becoming the first "techno unit" to grace the top of the chart since YMO's *Naughty Boys* twenty-five years prior.[2] Although *Game* did not approach the sales numbers of established J-pop superstars such as Utada Hikaru or R&B-inflected boy band Exile, Perfume found themselves compared to one of the most beloved Japanese acts of the past fifty years. On one TV segment reporting on Perfume's chart performance, the hosts gasped loudly when the YMO factoid was mentioned.

The rest of 2008 saw an acceleration of the momentum that had been building for Perfume since "Polyrhythm" appeared on the recycling advertisement. Two weeks after the release of

Game, the trio embarked on its first nationwide tour, playing large music venues to crowds of thousands. Long-running music program *Music Station* named Perfume a "Young Gun" artist, and soon the trio were appearing on variety shows and popular magazines (although, during the promotion of *Game*, the group still appeared on regional shows, including one in which a puppet served as co-host). In summer 2008, the group performed at numerous music festivals, including a return trip to Summer Sonic and its first appearance at the country's largest gathering, Rock in Japan Festival.

Perfume worked unrelentingly. In July 2008, the group released a new single called "Love the World," an intricate electropop number featuring harp notes, big 1980s-style drum kicks and synthesizers leading to a catchy, danceable hook, making it more radio-friendly than previous Perfume songs. "Love the World" joined *Game* in making history: it became the highest charting technopop single on the Oricon's singles chart since YMO's "Kimi ni mune kyun," which had landed at number two in 1983. "Love the World" beat it by hitting number one.

A few months later, Perfume landed its own TV variety show, *Perfume no Kininaruko-chan,* on Nippon TV—one of Japan's major nationwide networks. In the program, the women talked and joked with various *tarento* (television personalities), a time-honored tradition in Japanese broadcasting. In early November, they played a concert at the Budōkan—a coliseum best known for hosting the Beatles' concert in Japan and many big-name rock musicians thereafter. They ended the year with an appearance on NHK's annual New Year's Eve music program, *Kōhaku Uta Gassen*, which is perennially one of the most-watched programs in Japan. They performed the song that had shot the group to stardom—"Polyrhythm." But Perfume's influence did not stop there.

A Producer in Demand

The aughts had been tough on Suzuki Ami. Before the turn of the century, the J-pop artist had been on a quick rise to the top of Japan's music scene. Backed by Euro-dance-inspired tracks courtesy of Komuro Tetsuya, her singles routinely topped the charts, and her albums easily moved over a million units. At her peak, she was neck-to-neck with megastar Hamasaki Ayumi in terms of sales and visibility. She appeared poised to be one of the biggest Japanese stars of the new century.

But it all came to a screeching halt in 2000, when she was completely blacklisted from the Japanese entertainment industry. The president of her production company was found guilty of tax evasion, and subsequently artists were not receiving royalties. Suzuki's parents sued in an effort to free her from the label and won, only to find that entertainment companies no longer wanted to work with her.[3] For the next few years, she acted as an independent artist before finally landing back on a major imprint, but she was far from the heights she experienced in the late 1990s. Suzuki experimented with various sounds—European trance-pop, chirpy mid-tempo numbers—but nothing was advancing her career. In 2007, she called Nakata Yasutaka.

Suzuki was not the first (and will not be the last) artist to work with Nakata in an effort to transform her sound. As Perfume's status in Japan grew, Nakata's visibility as a producer rose in tandem, thanks to media focus on the trio's "new" sound. He began appearing in magazine and TV interviews, ranging from getting-to-know-you interviews to demonstrations of vocoders in a playhouse-like set. Nakata's other projects also received more media attention, of which Capsule (of which he was an actual member rather than a studio producer) found the biggest spotlight. By this time, the duo's music had shifted toward a Perfume-like sound, with neo-Shibuya-kei making way for a pounding electropop sound that took the bright joys of Perfume into the thrills of the club. Although Capsule catered to a niche market, its album *Flash Back,* released six months after "Polyrhythm," moved a then-best 37,915 copies—nearly 15,000 more units than its previous effort.

Nakata's services as a songwriter and producer became increasingly in demand, as acts, both fledgling and established, sought his magic electropop touch for a cool and contemporary edge. One of the first of these acts after Perfume began to rocket upward was of the singer and songwriter Meg, who also worked as a fashion designer and model. Prior to working with Nakata, Meg's music had moved around styles, from slowed-down R&B to stripped-down ballads, without much traction. On her spring 2007 album *Aquaberry*, she had worked with electronic producer i-dep (Nakamura Hiroshi)—in cuts such as "Now Released" and "Stars in the Blue Sky," the shuffling beats, synthesizer, and autotuned vocals. Having met Nakata through a fashion-designer friend,[4] Meg worked with him on two well-received singles and the album *Beam*, which redefined her sound toward technopop. Around this time, Suzuki also came to Nakata for a sonic makeover, releasing the double A-side single, "Free Free / Super Music Maker," to much critical praise. As *Game* became a hit in 2008, it raised the popularity of Nakata and the electropop sound further. Two months after *Game*, Meg's fifth album *Step,* her second with Nakata, debuted at number eight on Oricon, a career-high for her and making her the second technopop artist after Perfume to make the top ten. That November, Suzuki's *Supreme Show*, produced by Nakata, broke the top twenty; it was overshadowed a week later, when Capsule's tenth collection, *More! More! More!* reached number six, eventually selling over 67,000 copies.

The ultimate sign of Nakata's success came when Nakata was asked to write and produce the song "Kokoro Puzzle Rhythm" (2008) for SMAP. A boy band in the stable of Johnny's Associates, SMAP was one of Japan's most successful pop groups, with thirty-three number-one singles; it was a cultural institution, with a long-running weekly variety TV show, multiple radio shows, and many television and commercial appearances. For its eighteenth studio album, *Super Modern Artistic Performance*, SMAP featured Nakata's electropop alongside songs created by will.i.am of the Black-Eyed Peas and South Korea's Park Jin-young (JYP). When SMAP performed the song live on tours, the members played up its futuristic feel, with robotic choreography and wrap-around microphones that looked as if they were straight out of a sci-fi movie.

Electropop in the Mainstream

Working with SMAP topped a year in which Nakata and his style solidified their position within the J-pop industry. An exemplary compilation of this period was *Beautiful Techno* (July 2008), released at the peak of the electropop boom. The fifteen-track collection featured not only several Nakata-produced tracks (including Meg's "Amai Zeitaku," a reworking of a song by his longtime friend Ram Rider) but also artists like cheery duo Sweet Vacation and clear-voiced Immi, who were benefiting from the groundswell of interest in electropop. Other standouts included solo creators Aira Mitsuki and Saori@destiny, who were in part produced by Ōnishi Terukado, the founder of D-topia Entertainment, which carried some of the best electropop of the late aughts.

Many of the artists on *Beautiful Techno* found deals on major labels or large distributors. Yet despite the embrace of Perfume, they largely did not manage to crossover into the mainstream. Albums from Mitsuki and Saori@destiny sold just enough to enter the outer zone of the Oricon charts, while few others had much chance to sell to a wider audience. Although several performers went on to solid careers in niche markets, the electropop revolution did not come to J-pop. Even Nakata's other electropop projects—Meg and his own Capsule—started to see declining sales in subsequent years.

Instead, electropop saw itself replaced by a bigger media phenomenon. In October 2009, the idol group AKB48 landed their first number-one single on the Oricon charts, launching a renewed idol boom across the country. AKB48 retained many of the aspects of older idol groups—a sense of innocence, interchangeable members, a focus on connections with fans— but at an enormous scale. The group's membership—which then had only 48 members—now includes over 100 women, and elections were held to determine the positions of the members. Ballots were included in the CD singles, and many fans bought multiple copies of a single recording. As of June 2017, AKB48 had sold over 50 million records.[5] The producer behind the group, Akimoto Yasushi, also founded sister groups SKE48 (in Nagoya), NMB48 (Osaka), HKT48 (Fukuoka), NGT48 (Niigata), JKT48 (Jakarta), and SNH48 (Shanghai), as well as "rival" groups like Nogizaka46. The focus was not so much the music as the media spectacle and multipronged business model, which boosted demand for CDs, capturing most of the spots on the Oricon top-twenty charts and disengaging it from actual listening. Whereas Perfume had changed the soundscape of J-pop by launching an intriguing wave of mainstream electropop, Akimoto's groups retreated to familiar forms. Perfume stayed in the spotlight, but other electropop groups did not.

Digital Communities Get into the Act

Perfume and the electropop artists were not the only ones playing with technology. Online communities on Japanese video-sharing site Nico Nico Dōga (now Niconico) had already discovered Perfume before "Polyrhythm" catapulted them to fame. Some users created mash-ups and videos featuring their songs, while others did simple dance routines to their songs from the comfort of their bedrooms. Some of the earliest creations were footage of video game characters dancing while Perfume's "Electro World" played in the background. These user videos exposed Perfume's music to a wider online audience. It helped to shape the sounds that would become popular, not only on Niconico, but across online communities in Japan.[6]

Around the time that Perfume was gaining momentum in the summer of 2007, an updated version of a vocaloid, a singing-synthesizer software, arrived on store shelves. It allowed users to program a singing voice, composed of samples of a human singer. Sales of these programs skyrocketed when Japanese company Crypton Future Media put Hatsune Miku—a turquoise-haired, female character in anime style—on the box.[7] An online scene developed around Hatsune Miku, and while some tried to make her sound as human as possible (as the original developers of vocaloids had envisioned), many more users embraced the artificiality of Miku's sound. The simultaneous emergence of Perfume and vocaloids as popular forces in music is not a coincidence. Nakata's electronic manipulation of human voices can sound like vocaloid software, which gives anyone the chance to be a producer, even without access to a human singer. Japanese listeners and creators were embracing the electro world, including both pop stars and tools. Niconico, in which mash-ups of Perfume had already thrived, was a perfect place for Hatsune Miku's music to bloom.

Sweet Smell of Success

With the underdog stretch of Perfume's career having ended, Perfume solidified their position in the J-pop universe in 2009. Its second album, *Triangle*, was released in July 2009, topping the charts once again. This sophomore effort zipped between styles while keeping the electropop base, exploring disco, blog-house, and throwback technopop (on "Night Flight," which became another Pino ice cream commercial). Other tie-ups with cosmetic companies, alcohol brands, and Pepsi were also signed. Indeed, A-chan, Kashiyuka, and Nocchi were fixtures on not only commercials but Japanese television shows. Their live shows kept growing larger, hitting a milestone in 2010 when they played a sold-out show at Tokyo Dome, which has a capacity of 55,000. Perfume were now firmly in the upper tier of J-pop. Whether or not one lived in Tokyo, the suburbs, or the countryside, everyone seemed to know Perfume and could probably hum "Chocolate Disco."

Nakata Yasutaka was now a heavyweight J-pop producer. In addition to Perfume, Meg, and Capsule, he worked with many more artists. He produced more songs for SMAP, while also bringing his skills to rising rock band Scandal, R&B-pop

star Crystal Kay, and the 1980s "eternal idol" Matsuda Seiko. His international reputation appeared to also be growing, as he gained the rights to remix Australian superstar Kylie Minogue's 2010 number "Get Outta My Way." Nakata also played live at clubs, highlighted by a residency at Tokyo's Club Asia. But perhaps his most famous post-Perfume partnership is with Kyary Pamyu Pamyu (Takemura Kiriko). A former Tokyo fashion blogger and model on the streets of Harajuku, Tokyo's youth fashion capital, ventured into J-pop with Nakata as her sonic shepherd. In songs like her debut single, "PonPonPon" (July 2011), his floor-filling electropop was combined with inspiration from her playroom persona, with funky bass, galloping drums, and xylophones. The fresh sounds, combined with Kyary's fashion sense and a surreal-kawaii video, made the song a viral hit; it even captured Katy Perry's attention and brought her international attention.

Perfume's third album, *JPN* (November 2011), saw a continuation of their success, marking the group's third consecutive number-one album. In contrast to the eclecticism of *Triangle,* it had a more consistent electropop style. It was also the last album Perfume released on Tokuma before moving to Universal Music Japan, one of the big three international record labels. The move signaled the group's international ambitions.

7 Love the World

Austin's Highland Lounge was at full capacity minutes before Perfume was scheduled to take the stage for a performance at 1:00 a.m. It was one of the most anticipated shows at the 2015 South by Southwest Music Conference and Festival. Texas-based fans of the trio knew it would become a hot ticket. Since that morning, fans had been taking positions in lawn chairs outside the venue (one of Austin's largest gay nightclubs), and they had refused to budge for the next fifteen hours, ignoring the non-stop decadence of tech-company-sponsored parties and strategically taking turns to get provisions from Whole Foods. As the start of the show drew near, these people looked like geniuses. By midnight, getting in appeared impossible. Some friends stepped out around 11:30 p.m. to grab an artisanal sausage across the street, and when they came back an hour later, they were turned away.

About four minutes after the intended start time, a human tunnel formed near the entrance, and the three members of Perfume made their way to the stage, with the staff weaving through the crowd like a living barrier. Then the lights dimmed, and the show got underway. Owing to SXSW's reputation as a place where the latest interactive technology takes center stage, Perfume used their first show in Austin to show off eye-dazzling technology, live-streamed worldwide via YouTube (similar to YMO, which beamed its first-ever US show in Los Angeles to viewers back in Japan[1]). Users tuning in from their computers were treated to a dazzling performance, in which

A-chan, Kashiyuka, and Nocchi danced to a thumping new song called "Story," the stage backdrop changing nonstop from blueprints for a high-security building to a flurry of geometric shapes and colors. The live-stream stopped after "Story"—much to the chagrin of fans in Japan, some of who confessed on Twitter that they had taken the day off from work to watch the show. But the high-tech aspects of this performance generated the headlines. "Hot damn, this concert is straight out of the future," declared the headline on Wired's website,[2] recalling the impression that YMO had initially cultivated in the West.

But anyone who was at the Highland that night (and knew a bit more about Perfume) would have seen it differently. I was standing by the left side of the stage, between the men's bathroom and front door. From my vantage point, the group looked as if they were dancing with detached plastic doors. When the live-stream went off, the energy inside the venue really ramped up. For a Japan-based fan like myself, the atmosphere at this tiny club was a rare treat, as the group regularly sold out baseball stadiums. Once the gigantic visuals and top-of-the-line technological flourishes were gone, the atmosphere became intimate with fans only a few feet away from the members of Perfume. Everyone there appeared to be a die-hard fan of the group, from the people who drove down from Dallas, to the musicians who had played earlier that night as part of the showcase. They danced along to the entire seven-song set, which included songs from the length of Perfume's career. Any short breaks in sound were filled with fans screaming out the name of their favorite member. During the final number, "Chocolate Disco," the crowd shouted the chorus with all its might, as if everyone there had been waiting for years to release her pent-up energy.

Connecting Abroad

While Perfume had been widely covered in Japanese media since *Game*, the group had hardly received any coverage from English-language publications, particularly outside Japan. One of the only prominent English-language channels to cover Perfume had been the website *All Music,* for which Tokyo-based music journalist Ian Martin had reviewed *Game*.[3] Nonetheless, Perfume and Nakata had attracted a fan base beyond Japan. Web-based fan pages devoted to Perfume emerged well before the group had achieved mainstream success. A *LiveJournal* devoted to Nakata and the artists on his Contemode label appeared in September 2005: "Why love Contemode? Simple. They are on the cutting edge of cool, both visually and musically, combining elements of electropop, Shibuya-kei, French pop, acid jazz and lounge, and most recently, electro-disco, dance, and hardcore house."[4] As for Perfume, the English-language fan site *Perfume City* went live on June 1, 2006. As the first news post announced, "I didn't find anything in the net about Perfume, so I decided to compile info, romanize lyrics from booklets, search for images, scans and PVs . . . and here it is: *Perfume City*. I hope you find what you're searching for—if you're searching—or just take fun in the site." Other sites emerged as the group's profile grew, and some non-Japanese users uploaded videos of themselves dancing to Perfume or covering the group's songs.[5]

Initially, Perfume remained a niche interest internationally, despite the attention paid to *Game*. While global musicians have often had a more difficult time penetrating the US market than, say, the European markets, Japanese artists are also penalized for their labels' reluctance to make their videos widely available on YouTube overseas; in contrast,

South Korean labels have made K-Pop videos easily available. Nonetheless, fans, like those running Perfume City, found the music and information themselves, which entailed much work and persistence. Perfume City linked to any audiovisual clip or TV performance that they could find or offered downloads of music videos. This approach was unstable, as YouTube videos were often taken down after complaints from Japanese TV stations or other copyright holders.[6]

Despite all of these challenges, overseas fans of Perfume came together on blogs and message boards to share media related to the group and gush about the three performers. While overseas fans did talk about the music, they primarily felt a connection to the female singers, which is not very different from most Japanese fans. Looking at an "introduce yourself" thread on Perfume City, most participants seemed to be teenagers and twenty-somethings who already had an interest in Japanese pop culture, as well as fans of Japanese idols groups like Morning Musume or singers like Hamasaki Ayumi. Of the threads still visible online, many revolve around sharing pictures or interesting personal tidbits about A-chan, Kashiyuka, and Nocchi. When "Polyrhythm" landed in the top ten of the Oricon weekly chart, fans on Perfume City expressed how happy they were for the group, and thrilled for the trio for making their dreams come true. It was vital to these fans to follow Perfume's story from an unknown group to chart-topper.

Early Adopters

On the purely musical side of things, Nakata's creations with Perfume and his other assorted projects seemed in line with current trends. *Game*'s songs were in complete step with the vogue of dance sounds in the United States and England—maximal, pounding electropop, exemplified by the rise of French electronic duo Justice, and nu-rave, pushed forward by England's Klaxons. Yet the general inaccessibility of Japanese music ran counter to the ways in which music was being discovered and heard in other parts of the world. By 2008, blogs devoted to sharing mp3 files existed by the hundreds, while YouTube emerged as the place where artists reached new listeners.

Nonetheless, the music did reach some ears overseas. In a 2014 interview, Michael Angelakos, the founder and brains behind American dance-pop outfit Passion Pit, told me: "I remember my friend showing me [the Capsule song] 'Eternity' one night in Boston, I think it was late 2007 or 2008. Something like that. That was a moment that made me both want to make music immediately that very second and feel defeated, wanting to quit music entirely." He bought as many Nakata-produced tracks as he could find, leading him to find first Meg and Suzuki Ami, and then Perfume. "They, at least to me, represent a hyper-modern take on girl groups that flooded the market in the nineties, and now he's taking that and spinning it in such a unique way that I find simply irresistible. I've always just loved the music, but conceptually it manages to be both meticulously executed and really fun."[7]

Passion Pit was one of the first projects to adopt musical ideas from Nakata's sounds. As Angelakos explained, "I'm pretty sure I was listening to Capsule every day during the making of *Manners*." Passion Pit's first full-length album, *Manners* (2009) catapulted the group into a festival mainstay, ever present in commercials. He acknowledged, "Most of my left-of-center approaches are at least influenced by Nakata's energy, if not other elements." This influence can be heard in his music, which features a flurry of interlocking synthesizer melodies that give Passion Pit's music a warm, emotional feeling (although Angelakos' singing is nowhere near as processed as Perfume's). Outside of Passion Pit, however, Nakata and Perfume's influence remained relatively scant outside of Japan, as of the end of the aughts. The next global wave of EDM revealed how widely appealing their brand of electropop could become. They were ahead of their time.

Electronic dance music, or EDM for short, is a catch-all phrase referring to electronically generated music, usually with a thumping four-to-the-floor beat, for dancing at clubs and raves. Beginning with electro, techno, and house in the 1980s, EDM has grown to encompass a dizzying array of subgenres. EDM had enjoyed a boom in Europe (and to a lesser extent in Japan) for decades, but according to Simon Reynolds, it was only in the late 2000s that the US music industry began to promote EDM heavily, pushing "EDM" to refer to a new generation of rave music at festivals.[8] Part of this boom was due to the worldwide popularity of Daft Punk. As with other regions, the primary attraction of EDM was the live event. By the late aughts, the internet had made it easy to listen to many kinds of music, particularly through YouTube or Blogspot, some posting on which offered files ready to be downloaded. Everything could be discovered with adroit googling. This easy accessibility helped to erase the unspoken lines among disparate scenes; listeners could simultaneously love indie rock, rap, and French house without attracting many raised eyebrows. The producers behind EDM events could be similar eclectic. A typical EDM festival set could easily jump among sonic worlds, with house blending into drum 'n' bass into a thundering Southern trap cut.

When EDM finally began to attract mainstream attention in the United States, Nakata's musical influence outside Japan became evident. Festival headliners such as Porter Robinson mentioned his name as a major influence, while the EDM songs heard on mainstream radio bore a striking resemblance to the catchy electropop that Nakata had mastered throughout his career. One of the earliest viral videos associated with the EDM scene was by the eighteen-year-old French artist Madeon (Hugo Pierre Leclercq). In the clip, he performed the song "Pop Culture" live, his fingers moving rapidly over a Novation Launchpad, the controller used with the Ableton Live production software. The song mashed pieces of thirty-nine songs Leclercq liked (as he himself announced in the introduction preceding the video), including Daft Punk, Linkin Park, the Buggles, Britney Spears, and Michael Jackson. Among this whirlwind could be heard a sample of Capsule's 2009 song, "Can I Have a Word," a string-heavy number that is one of Nakata's most refined electropop bouncers. Its subtle inclusion was an early sign of what was to come.

Leclercq had first came across Nakata's work in 2008 through the Capsule album *More! More! More!* before discovering *Game.* As he explained in a 2015 interview for Japanese music website *Natalie,*

> The way [Nakata] arranges chords (harmonies) is very intelligent and complex, but at the same time, it's pop. That's what makes it so original, and what really blew my mind. Most western pop is very simple and easy to understand. Nakata's music adds intelligence to the mix. . . . For example, Perfume's "Polyrhythm" takes a difficult and complicated rhythm, and adorns it with a pop melody that anyone could enjoy. That's

what makes it so amazing. His skill in chord progressions and melody composition. . . .[9]

Nakata's influence on Madeon can be seen on his debut album *Adventure* (2015). In "Pay No Mind," synthesizers punctuate harmonies and play plaintive melodies; in "Beings," 8-bit sound and voice samples mix with electropop bass; and a funky electrified bass dominates the track "Imperium." He subscribes to a maximal aesthetic that makes the most of every available digital inch, but he also weaves in a warm melody—both qualities reminiscent of Nakata's approach.

Well before *Adventure* became a commercial and critical success, the Russian producer Zedd (Anton Zaslavski) created "Spectrum," his debut single. As in Madeon's work, the main vocal (sung by Matthew Koma) seems relatively untouched and hints at the dramatic direction he would later pursue in "Clarity" and "Break Free," the latter of which he wrote for pop star Ariana Grande. "Spectrum" reminds the listener of Nakata, particularly in the instrumentals following each hook: the seventh and ninth chords one hears in Perfume's "Baby Cruising Love" or "Ceramic Girl," or the synthesizer timbres of the latter, are heard here. The main riff is adorned by numerous melodic fills, with the instruments sometimes dropping out in silence at climactic moments. "Spectrum" performed well on dance charts worldwide and received plenty of radio play; it is one of the best-known tracks that sounds indebted to Capsule.

Many producers (and fans) who came of age in the 1990s have a common entry point into Japanese popular culture: video games. In the 1990s and 2000s, Japanese popular culture was widely accepted among Western youth, who played *Pokémon, Zelda,* or *Final Fantasy* and watched anime like *Cowboy Bebop* or *Neon Genesis Evangelion*.[10]

With the popularity of these franchises, Japan had become cool. Porter Robinson, a North Carolina-born producer, was influenced by *Dance Dance Revolution*, a rhythm-based arcade and home video game by Konami from Japan. The game sparked his interest in Japanese pop music, which led him to Nakata. He said,

> I think that he is a master of doing much of what I want to do. He writes stuff in a poppy format with hooks and bridges and verses but they're always quirky and captivating. I think that a lot of Western pop, especially from the Swedish masters of pop writing, much of it feels cold and cynical and zoned in, in a lot of ways. Nakata's music is always soulful, charming and expressive in some way.[11]

At the beginning of his career, Robinson produced EDM tracks in the predictable but successful pattern of slow builds, then rapid bass. With "Language" (2012), he began to include a sweet, lithe synthesizer melody alongside the pounding bass line. In sound and affect, "Language" seemed to draw from Nakata. In *Worlds* (2014), Robinson reacted to the hard-hitting, one-dimensional feel of EDM. This album's sounds were inspired by J-pop and Nakata, with colorful synthesizer lines, catchy hooks, vocaloid technology, and technopop-like ideas. With *Worlds*, Robinson became the most publicly visible artist in a primarily online scene of Japanophiles who like J-pop, upload cuddly *anime*-style drawings for their album artwork, and unironically love *kawaii* (cuteness). Perfume and Nakata are still far from being known by most music fans in the States, but a very large number of producers—bedroom-based or otherwise—have found their music and become inspired. The songs they create are maximal, bouncy, and full of different sounds. And critically, they feature the same emotionality as the songs on *Game*. As Robinson said, "I think probably the most straightforward way to explain his genius is to say that he uses pop format and almost-pop chords but he uses crazy, technical jazz chords and goes to the craziest moods but still makes it work. . . . He gives his music a very unique character. It's really the most genius pop ever."[12]

New Age, Similar Story

International attention to Perfume picked up through exposure to mainstream media. The first big breakthrough came when Pixar's John Lasseter chose "Polyrhythm" to appear in the 2011 animated film *Cars 2*. Although only a brief snippet of the song appeared during a scene set in Tokyo, the song was included in full on the official soundtrack album; moreover, the trio was invited to Hollywood for the world premiere of the film. Standing on the red carpet, Lasseter claimed, "The moment I listened to 'Polyrhythm,' I loved it, it was like falling in love."[13] This brief trip to Los Angeles served as a catalyst to a greater push abroad. Perfume signed with Universal Music Japan, allowing greater access to non-Japanese markets. Fans who once had to dig deep to find a thirty-second clip could simply access the official Perfume YouTube channel to watch high-quality videos. International shows soon followed, first across Asia (including Ultra Korea, an EDM-centric gathering), then to Europe and the United States.

When Perfume traveled to the West, the international press described the group as "futuristic" and "technologic." This result was intended; as Universal managing director Katō Kimitaka told Reuters in 2012, the label played on an image of "mysterious, futuristic, robotic, doll-type girls."[14] First, this image was in line with the one that Perfume had cultivated in Japan since "Linear Motor Girl" in 2005; there, the media had de-emphasized the futuristic angle once Perfume had established itself, with interviews focusing on the personalities, lifestyles, hobbies, and thoughts on new songs of the three women. But the positioning also played on Western perceptions of Japan as an ultra-modern place with cutting-edge technology—in some ways, a less ironic version of YMO's playing to the Western fantasy of the techno-oriental. Perfume's embrace of dazzling high-tech performances cemented this hyper-technological image overseas. For their show at the Cannes Lions International Festival of Creativity, fans downloaded 3D models of the women and submitted their own designs, which were projected during the dance. It is hence no wonder that the headlines for the Austin show emphasized "the future," or that much of international press coverage of Perfume worked on angles related to digital technology.

Although the press may have framed the group as a techno-orientalist fantasy, and many blog posts cast the women as robots rather than humans, I also think back to that show in Austin, watching several hundred people get swept up in the electropop the trio delivered. Perfume and the audience engaged in a display of emotional connection that felt very real. That sense of connection is part of what makes Perfume a special group in the history of J-pop. For many fans, *Game* served as the gateway into this music. That album's high-tech touches seemed ahead of its time at its release in 2008, and its digitally altered vocals and dazzling arrays of synthesizer melodies continue to make it sound futuristic, nearly ten years later. Nothing in Japanese pop sounded like it back then, and in my opinion, it stands as the last major stylistic leap in the country's mainstream-pop landscape.

Yet for all of its technological flair, it is the emotion at the core of *Game*—in the lyrics, the harmonies, and the women's performances—that makes the music connect with listeners, in Japan and elsewhere, and turns Perfume's debut album into a pop masterclass. The trio and Nakata took sounds that were unabashedly artificial and found the human heart within them. What could have been just a set of cool-sounding noises became resonant songs about love and one's place in the world, rendered through the buzzy and busy realities of the 2000s. *Game* and Perfume offer a ray of light for pop music in the new century, showing that thrilling new styles can break through even in the most conservative music markets, and that even the most digitized songs can inspire the truest feelings.

Notes

Introduction

1 Nakata is one of a long line of male producers behind pop artists, especially female ones; the most recent example is Akimoto Yasushi, the producer behind AKB48. See Carolyn Stevens, *Japanese Popular Music: Culture, Authenticity, and Power* (New York: Routledge, 2008).

2 *Perfume Locks* (2010), [Radio Program] Tokyo FM, September 23, 2010. Recording and English translation at https://www.youtube.com/watch?v=GKQ3l2KxlWk

3 *Oricon News*, "Perfume ga 1 kurai kakutoku! YMO irai yaku 25 nenburi no kaikyo!" April 22, 2008, http://www.oricon.co.jp/news/53959/full/

4 Ibid.

5 Ian Martin, "Decade of Fine Tuning Yields Gold for Capsule," *Japan Times*, June 3, 2011, www.japantimes.co.jp/culture/2011/06/03/music/decade-of-fine-tuning-yields-gold-for-capsule/

6 "Zero nendai ni futatabi 'technopop' būmu o *yomigaerasete Perfume no kōzai*," *Aerodynamik*, March 30, 2010, http://aerodynamik.hatenablog.com/entry/20100330/p1

7 "Sakamoto Ryūichi, dai 21 kai 'ongaku' ni tsuite iikiru," *Openers*, April 11, 2011, http://openers.jp/article/10960

8 Hosokawa Shūhei, "Soy Sauce Music: Haruomi Hosono and Japanese Self-Orientalism," in *Widening the Horizon: Exoticism in Post-War Popular Music,* ed. Philip Hayward (Bloomington, IN: Indiana University Press, 1999), 114–44.

9   David S. Roh, Betsy Huang, and Greta A. Niu, "Technologizing Orientalism: An Introduction," in *Techno-Orientalism: Imagining Asia in Speculative Fiction, History, and Media* (New Brunswick: Rutgers University Press, 2015), 2.

1: The Age of Technopop

1   Tanaka Akiko, "Watashi no ichi-mai: 4-ninme no YMO to yobareta otoko no senjō: Matsutake Hideki-san," *Asahi Digital & Men*, March 27, 2017, http://www.asahi.com/and_M/articles/SDI2017032420091.html.

2   Onada Yū, "Isao Tomita: Moog Reverie," *Resident Advisor*, July 13, 2012, https://www.residentadvisor.net/features/1586

3   Jordan Ferguson and Ichijō Yūko, "Isao Tomita: Switched On," *Red Bull Music Academy*, 2014, http://daily.redbullmusicacademy.com/enhanced/isao-tomita-comic-

4   Emmanuelle Loubet, "The Beginnings of Electronic Music in Japan, with a Focus on the NHK Studio: The 1950s and 1960s," *Computer Music Journal, 21/4* (1997), 11–12.

5   Onada, "Isao Tomita."

6   Michael K. Bourdaghs, *Sayonara Amerika, Sayonara Nippon: A Geopolitical Prehistory of J-Pop* (New York: Columbia University Press, 2012), 186–92.

7   *POSTYMO* (2008), [DVD] Japan: Commmons.

8   Tom Ewing, "Kraftwerk, the Catalog Review," *Pitchfork*, December 1, 2009, http://pitchfork.com/reviews/albums/13742-the-catalogue/

9   Andrew Stout, "Yellow Magic Orchestra on Kraftwerk and
       How to Write a Melody during a Cultural Revolution,"
       SF Weekly, June 24, 2011, http://www.sfweekly.com/
       shookdown/2011/06/24/yellow-magic-orchestra-on-
       kraftwerk-and-how-to-write-a-melody-during-a-cultural-
       revolution

10   *Nippon sengo subculture shi* [TV Program], NHK, September
       5, 2014

11   W. David Marx, "The Plastics and Copy Anxiety,"
       Neojaponisme, March 1, 2016, http://neojaponisme.
       com/2016/03/01/the-plastics-and-copy-anxiety/

12   *Chwet* [blog], "P-Model and Hikashū *Music Night Talk*
       Interview," June 15, 2016, https://chwet.wordpress.
       com/2016/06/15/p-model-and-hikashu-music-night-talk-
       interview/. English translation of *Music Night Talk* radio
       program, FM Tokyo, March 31, 1980.

13   Mima Akiko, *The Dig Presents Disc Guide Series: Techno Pop*
       (Tokyo: Shinko Music Publishing Ltd., 2004).

14   Ibid., 30.

2: Music Controller

1   *Sound & Recording* [Magazine], "Interview with Nakata
       Yasutaka and Sakamoto Ryūichi," November 2012.

2   *Sound & Recording* [Magazine], "Interview with Nakata
       Yasutaka and Oda Tetsurō," June 2013.

3   Roh et al., *Techno-Orientalism*, 8.

4   *Sound & Recording,* "Nakata and Sakamoto."

5   Elizabeth Lazarowitz, "His Techno-Pop Is Big in Japan, But
       Will It Play Here?" *The Los Angeles Times,* November 5, 1997

http://articles.latimes.com/1997/nov/05/business/fi-50370;
James Bates, "Murdoch Ventures into Music Business," *Los
Angeles Times*, December 7, 1996. http://articles.latimes.
com/1996-12-07/business/fi-6533_1_major-music

6   *Sound & Recording* [Magazine], "Interview with Nakata
     Yasutaka and Komuro Tetsuya," October 2011.

7   *Fuck Yeah Yasutaka Nakata* [blog], "Biography," November 4,
     2015, http://fuckyeahystk.tumblr.com/biography

8   Ian Martin, "Refashioning the J-Pop Scene," *Japan
     Times*, August 21, 2009, www.japantimes.co.jp/
     culture/2009/08/21/music/refashioning-the-J-pop-scene/

9   W. David Marx, "The Legacy of Shibuya-Kei Part Five,"
     Neojaponisme, November 22, 2004, http://neojaponisme.
     com/2004/11/22/the-legacy-of-shibuya-kei-part-five/

10   Martin, "Refashioning J-Pop."

11   Mori Itsuki, "Interview with Nakata Yasutaka," *Quick Japan*,
     October 12, 2007.

3: A New Scent

1   Philosoranter, "30 Shocking Legends of Perfume," *Perfume
     City*, accessed July 4, 2017, http://www.perfume-city.com/
     info/30legends/. English translation of *Flash Magazine*, "30
     Shocking Legends of Perfume," June 17, 2008.

2   *Perfume Locks* [Radio Program], Tokyo FM, August 19, 2010.
     Recording and English translation, https://www.youtube.
     com/watch?v=ZiPTuS7KOto

3   Ibid.

4   Philosoranter, *Flash Magazine*.

5   Sharon Kinsella, "Cuties in Japan," in *Women, Media and
     Consumption in Japan*, ed. Brian Moeran and Lise Skov (New

York: Routledge, 2013), 220–54. First published by Curzon, 1995.

6   Aoyagi Hiroshi, "The Making of Japanese Adolescent Role Models," *Islands of Eight Million Smiles: Idol Performance and Symbolic Production in Contemporary Japan* (Cambridge, MA: Harvard University Asia Center, 2005), 56–85.

7   Ibid.

8   Christopher Howard, "National Idols? The Problem of 'Transnationalizing' Film Stardom in Japan's Idol Economy," in *East Asian Film Stars*, ed. Leung Wing-Fai and Andy Willis (Palgrave Macmillan UK, 2014), 49–64.

9   J. Fukunishi, "Japan '65: Electric Guitars Twang, the Ventures Clang," *Billboard Magazine*, January 15, 1966.

10   Brian Ashcraft and Ueda Shōko, *Japanese Schoolgirl Confidential: How Teenage Girls Made a Nation Cool* (Tokyo: Tuttle Publishing, 2014), 38–39.

11   Ibid.

12   Aoyagi, *Islands of Eight Million Smiles*, 67–68.

13   Ashcraft and Ueda, *Japanese Schoolgirl Confidential*, 44.

14   Aoyagi Hiroshi, "Following the Trajectory of an Idol Superstar," *Islands of Eight Million Smiles: Idol Performance and Symbolic Production in Contemporary Japan* (Cambridge, MA: Harvard University Asia Center, 2005), 166–203.

15   Patrick W. Galbraith and Jason G. Karlin, "Introduction: The Mirror of Idols and Celebrity," *Idols and Celebrity in Japanese Media Culture* (New York: Palgrave Macmillan, 2012), 1–32.

16   Yoshida Gō, "CD/DVD Complete Guide," *Music Magazine* 40/10, October 2008, 33.

17   Takemiya Keishi and uranothegod, "Sweet Donuts English Translation," *Perfume City*, http://perfume-city.com/lyrics/62/Sweet%20Doughnut/

18   taka02, "Vitamin Drop English Translation," *Perfume City*, http://www.perfume-city.com/lyrics/110/Vitamin%20Drop/

4: Brave New World

1   *Pa Pa Pa Pa Pa Pa Perfume* (2006), [TV Program], Enta!371, September 6, 2006.

2   *Perfume Locks* (2010), [Radio Program] Tokyo FM, September 30, 2010. Recording and English translation, https://www.youtube.com/watch?v=DrM2uSY-__A

3   Ibid.

4   Mori, "Nakata."

5   Eric Ducker, "Daft Punk: The Creators," *The Fader*, February 2007, http://www.thefader.com/2013/06/28/daft-punk-the-creators

6   *Fuck Yeah Yasutaka Nakata* [blog], "Why Did Nakata Change His Style?," December 21, 2015. http://fuckyeahystk.tumblr.com/post/135689915717

7   *School of Electro* [blog], "Capsule 'FRUITS CLiPPER' Interview @ Traksy (August – September 2006)," accessed July 4, 2017, http://schoolofelectro.tumblr.com/post/145035063349. English translation of interview on *trasky* [Web Site].

8   Ryou, "Computer City Translated," *Perfume City*, http://www.perfume-city.com/lyrics/21/Computer%20City/

9   Yūta, "Electro World Translated," *Perfume City*, http://www.perfume-city.com/lyrics/15/Electro%20World/

10   oneoffrfmfansinjpn, "Chocolate Disco Translated," *Perfume City*, http://www.perfume-city.com/lyrics/101/Chocolate%20Disco/

11 *Oh! My Radio* [Radio Program], J-Wave, March 27, 2007, English translation, https://www.youtube.com/watch?v=W5JPEy84Df8

12 *Perfume Locks* [Radio Program], Tokyo FM, October 7, 2010. Recording and English translation, https://www.youtube.com/watch?v=06H149UprVM

13 *Oh! My Radio.*

14 *Natalie* [Web Site], "[Perfume] Kōkyō kōkoku kikō CM ni shutsuen! Shinkyoku mo hirō." June 23, 2007, http://natalie.mu/music/news/2336

15 Mori, "Nakata."

16 aniota, "Perfume 'Poririzumu' ga Orikon Uiikurii Chaato 7-i ranku-in," *Ex* (blog), September 18, 2007, http://aniota.hatenablog.jp/entry/20070918/1190094211.

5: Play the Game

1 Mori, "Nakata."

2 *Quick Japan*, "Perfume Article," December 10, 2007.

3 Munetaka Akimasa, "Nakata Yasutaka Feature," *Music Magazine*, October 2008.

4 *Quick Japan*, "Perfume Article," December 10, 2007.

5 Mori, "Nakata."

6 Ibid.; Takahashi Osamu, "Kashiyuka, Nocchi, A-chan: San-nin awasete Paafyūmu desu," *Music Magazine*, October 2008, 40–43.

7 *Top Runner* [TV Program], "Perfume Episode," NHK, April 2008, https://www.youtube.com/watch?v=M-SKINp6Kc0

8   *My 10 Golden Rules* [TV Program], "Nakata Yasutaka,"
     TBS, September 8, 2009 https://www.youtube.com/
     watch?v=5WMyjU5RweU. Other DJs like DJ Krush have
     also described the production process as similar to cooking.
     See Noriko Manabe, "Representing Japan: 'National' Style
     among Japanese Hip-Hop DJs," *Popular Music* 32/1 (2013),
     35–50.

9   Mori, "Nakata."

10   Ibid.

11   Ibid.

12   Galbraith and Karlin, *Idols and Celebrity*, 1–2.

13   *Perfume Fan Service by TV. Bros.*, "2008 Special: Perfume,
     Let's Play the Game," Tokyo News Mook, October 1, 2015.
     The editor thanks Julia Sanua (Temple University) for her
     insight in pointing out this play on words. Duncan Cooper
     and Toshio Masuda, "Interview: Kyary Pamyu Pamyu," *The
     Fader,* April 13, 2013, http://www.thefader.com/2013/04/16/
     interview-kyary-pamyu-pamyu

6: Take Off

1   *Oricon News*, "2008 Year-End Album Ranking," 2008, http://
     contents.oricon.co.jp/music/special/081211_01_03.html

2   *Oricon News*, "Perfume ga 1 kurai kakutoku! YMO irai yaku 25
     nenburi no kaikyo!" April 22, 2008, http://www.oricon.co.jp/
     news/53959/full/

3   Robert Michael Poole, "You and Whose Ami?," *Japan
     Times*, November 20, 2008, http://www.japantimes.
     co.jp/culture/2008/11/20/music/you-and-whose-ami/#.
     V61spbVA07B

4   *School of Electro* [blog], "MEG 'OK' Interview @ Hotexpress (October 2007)," accessed July 4, 2017, http://schoolofelectro.tumblr.com/post/144526892244. English translation of interview on *Hotexpress*, October 2007.

5   Takahashi Osamu, "*Game,*" Top Albums of the Aughts List, *Music Magazine*, July 7, 2010

6   *Oricon News*, "AKB 48, 35-saku renzoku ichi-i & 30 sakumoku mirion CD sō uriage 5000 man-mai toppa," June 6, 2017, http://www.oricon.co.jp/news/2091907/full/

7   Patrick St. Michel, "The Making of Vocaloid," *Red Bull Music Academy*, November 11, 2014, http://daily.redbullmusicacademy.com/2014/11/vocaloid-feature; Keisuke Yamada, *Supercell's Supercell ft. Hatsune Miku* (New York: Bloomsbury, 2017).

7: Love the World

1   Ed Harrison, "Yellow Magic U.S. Show Will Beam Live to Japan," *Billboard Magazine*, November 1, 1980.

2   Kyle Vanhemert, "Hot Damn, This Concert Is Straight Out of the Future," *Wired*, March 23, 2015, http://www.wired.com/2015/03/hot-damn-concert-straight-future/

3   Ian Martin, "*Game* Review," *All Music*, 2008, http://www.allmusic.com/album/game-mw0001247918

4   Contemode, About Page, *Contemode LiveJournal*, September 12, 2005, http://contemode.livejournal.com/profile?admins=owner

5   jigenbakuda, "Perfume Fans Around the World," *Perfume City*, June 17, 2008, http://www.perfume-city.com/2008/06/17/perfume-fans-around-the-world/

6   ekuseru, "New Media," *Perfume City*, October 10, 2006, http://www.perfume-city.com/2006/10/10/new-media/

7   Patrick St. Michel, "Perfume are Poised To Make It In America," *Wondering Sound*, November 24, 2014, http://webcache.googleusercontent.com/search?q=cache:ygooGUs3 IFUJ:www.wonderingsound.com/feature/perfume-j-pop-passion-pit/+&cd=1&hl=en&ct=clnk&gl=jp

8   Simon Reynolds, "How Rave Music Conquered America," *Guardian*, August 2, 2012, https://www.theguardian.com/music/2012/aug/02/how-rave-music-conquered-america

9   Murakami Hisashi, "Madeon X Nakata Yasutaka," *Natalie*, July 1, 2015, http://natalie.mu/music/pp/madeon_yasutaka

10 See Rose Bridges, *Yōko Kanno's Cowboy Bebop* (New York: Bloomsbury, 2017), for more information on anime music.

11 Sam Murphy, "Porter Robinson: 'I'm Not Changing to Make a Million Dollars,'" *Music Feeds*, August 8, 2014, http://musicfeeds.com.au/features/porter-robinson-im-not-changing-to-make-a-million-dollars/

12 Ibid.

13 Daniel Robson, "Will the World Soon Wake Up to the Scent of Perfume?," *Japan Times*, May 18, 2012, http://www.japantimes.co.jp/culture/2012/05/18/music/will-the-world-soon-wake-up-to-the-scent-of-perfume/

14 Mike Collett-White, "Label Scents Global Success with Japan Band Perfume," *Reuters*, March 7, 2012, http://www.reuters.com/article/us-japan-band-idUSTRE8260S520120308

Suggested Further Reading

Aoyagi, Hiroshi. *Islands of Eight Million Smiles: Idol Performance and Symbolic Production in Contemporary Japan*. Cambridge, MA: Harvard University Asia Center, 2005.

Ashcraft, Brian, and Ueda Shōko. *Japanese Schoolgirl Confidential: How Teenage Girls Made a Nation Cool*. Tokyo: Tuttle Publishing, 2014.

Bourdaghs, Michael K. *Sayonara Amerika, Sayonara Nippon: A Geopolitical Prehistory of J-Pop*. New York: Columbia University Press, 2012.

Bridges, Rose. *Yōko Kanno's Cowboy Bebop*. New York: Bloomsbury, 2017.

Galbraith, Patrick W., and Jason G. Karlin. "Introduction: The Mirror of Idols and Celebrity," *Idols and Celebrity in Japanese Media Culture*, 1–32. New York: Palgrave Macmillan, 2012.

Hosokawa, Shuhei. "Soy Sauce Music: Haruomi Hosono and Japanese Self-Orientalism." In *Widening the Horizon: Exoticism in Post-War Popular Music*, edited by Philip Hayward, 114–44. Bloomington, IN: Indiana University Press, 1999.

Howard, Christopher. "National Idols? The Problem of 'Transnationalizing' Film Stardom in Japan's Idol Economy." In *East Asian Film Stars*, edited by Leung Wing-Fai and Andy Willis, 49–64. New York: Palgrave Macmillan, 2014.

Kinsella, Sharon. "Cuties in Japan." In *Women, Media and Consumption in Japan*, edited by Brian Moeran and Lise Skov, 220–54. New York: Routledge, 2013. First published by Curzon, 1995.

Loubet, Emmanuelle. "The Beginnings of Electronic Music in Japan, with a Focus on the NHK Studio: The 1950s and 1960s." *Computer Music Journal*, 21/4 (1997), 11–22.

Manabe, Noriko. "Representing Japan: 'National' Style among Japanese Hip-Hop DJs," *Popular Music*, 32/1 (2013), 35–50.

Mima, Akiko. *The Dig Presents Disc Guide Series: Techno Pop*. Tokyo: Shinko Music Publishing Ltd., 2004.

Roh, David S., Betsy Huang, and Greta A. Niu. "Technologizing Orientalism: An Introduction." In *Techno-Orientalism: Imagining Asia in Speculative Fiction, History, and Media*, 1–19. New Brunswick: Rutgers University Press, 2015.

Stevens, Carolyn S. *Japanese Popular Music: Culture, Authenticity and Power*. Routledge Media, Culture and Social Change in Asia. New York: Routledge, 2008.

Tanaka, Yūji. *Denshi ongaku in Japan*. Tokyo: Asupekuto, 2001.

Yamada, Keisuke. *Supercell's Supercell ft. Hatsune Miku*. New York: Bloomsbury, 2017.

Index

Index